Workplace Vagabonds

Career and Community in
Changing Worlds of Work

Christina Garsten

palgrave
macmillan

First published 2008 by
PALGRAVE MACMILLAN

Palgrave Macmillan in the UK is an imprint of Macmillan Publishers Limited, registered in England, company number 785998, of Houndmills, Basingstoke, Hampshire RG21 6XS.

Palgrave Macmillan in the US is a division of St Martin's Press LLC, 175 Fifth Avenue, New York, NY 10010.

Palgrave Macmillan is the global academic imprint of the above companies and has companies and representatives throughout the world.

Palgrave® and Macmillan® are registered trademarks in the United States, the United Kingdom, Europe and other countries.

ISBN-13: 978-1-4039-1758-4 hardback
ISBN-10: 1-4039-1758-2 hardback

This book is printed on paper suitable for recycling and made from fully managed and sustained forest sources. Logging, pulping and manufacturing processes are expected to conform to the environmental regulations of the country of origin.

A catalogue record for this book is available from the British Library.

A catalog record for this book is available from the Library of Congress.

10 9 8 7 6 5 4 3 2 1
17 16 15 14 13 12 11 10 09 08

Printed and bound in Great Britain by
CPI Antony Rowe, Chippenham and Eastbourne

Contents

Acknowledgements

When I started the research for this book I too, was in some ways a 'temp'. As an academic, I had spent years working on temporary contracts. It was during the writing-up part of this study that I became a 'regular'. So, whilst I was studying 'the temps' of Stockholm, Leeds and Santa Clara, I could relate to much of what they told me. An increasing number of people, well-educated as well as less educated, today know what it means to be temporarily employed. I believe the stories and experiences of the temporary employees I met during my research have a relevance that goes beyond the particularities of temping, that connects quite closely with those of others working on different kinds of temporary contracts. As such, they may tell us something significant about the modern worlds of work.

For this winding journey across temping fields to come to completion, I am grateful to a number of people. First of all, I am grateful to the managers and assignment co-ordinators at Olsten Staffing Services for opening the doors for me, allowing me to move around in their offices, talk to their consultants, and meet them at their workplaces. The many client organizations that generously allowed me in have also contributed in significant ways. I also wish to thank representatives of the branch associations and the trade unions for assisting me with access to information and for constructive and interesting discussions along the way. To all the temps I have met during this venture I owe the greatest gratitude. Although you are not visible here by name, I have seen your faces and heard your voices all through the writing of this book. I have learnt a great deal through our encounters, and I can only hope I have been able to do you justice here.

In my own work environment, I have benefited greatly from 'jumping' between two dynamic research environments: Stockholm Center for Organizational Research (Score) and the Department of Social Anthropology, both at Stockholm University. I am grateful for constructive comments and inspiration from all my colleagues in these environments throughout the research process. Not least, thanks to Renita Thedvall and Jessica Lindvert, who have been sharing journeys as well as investigations into worklife cultures for quite some time now. In parallel to working on this project, I was engaged in exploring the trope of 'employability' together with Kerstin Jacobsson. The employability project, which resulted in the edited volume *Learning to be Employable* (2004), surely infused some ideas into this book. Thank you, Kerstin, for much fun and stimulating moments of collaboration!

Thanks also to Bengt Jacobsson and Kerstin Sahlin for supporting this project from the start, and to Nils Brunsson and Göran Ahrne for bringing out new aspects of the organization and regulation of temporary work. And Jan Turtinen, thanks for your energy and carefulness in the first round of interviews in the UK. With Staffan Furusten I tested the similarities and differences between temping and consulting, which proved most valuable for the sharpening of ideas. I owe a big thanks to Ida Seing for swiftly organizing some basic facts in the finalizing of this book. Had it not been for the patient support and wise inquiries of Ulf Hannerz, I wonder if this book would still have been a few pages away from completion. Monica Lindh de Montoya, Anna Hasselström, Hans Hedlund, Helena Wulff, Galina Lindquist and Gudrun Dahl – directly or indirectly you have also made working on this book more joyful. In other words, work places, as well as work communities and colleagues, matter a great deal!

Among colleagues and friends outside of my immediate habitats who have contributed their constructive ideas and critical voices along the road, I would like to thank in particular Chris Grey for long-term friendship and an always critical eye, Tor Hernes for always insisting on the potentiality of things, and Bas Koene for a keen ear and constructive ideas. At an early stage in the project, I was lucky to get involved in the book project *After Full Employment* run from the European University Institute in Florence. Here I met with Bo Stråth, who broadened my views at an early stage and Bénédicte Zimmermann, who has since shared my interests in the transformation of worklife as colleague and friend. I have greatly valued the haven of scholarly broadmindedness that the Scancor centre at Stanford University provides. It is during some of my stays here that this book was eventually written. Thanks to Barbara Beuche, Jim March and Woody Powell for stimulating periods of work and good ideas. Exchanges at the wider orbits of academic movement are often just as significant!

This project has been generously supported by The Swedish Research Council (Vetenskapsrådet) and Swedish Council for Working Life and Social Research (Forskningsrådet för arbetsliv och socialvetenskap). I would like to thank here as well Wendy Davies for her careful language editing and Jackie Kippenberger and Virginia Thorp at Palgrave Macmillan for their professionalism, their patience and commitment.

Those who know best what it takes to live with an academic vagabond, who have experienced the benefits and the flip sides of being flexible, jumping around, moving about, and writing it all up, are my family. Thank you Erik, for trusting me in testing the limits of flexibility, Tobias, for asking the significant questions, and Andreas, for introducing me to the superhero movie character The Elastigirl[1] of the Incredible Family, on assignment by the National Supers Agency. I confess to wishing I was her – occasionally.

CHRISTINA GARSTEN

Note

1. Helen Parr, whose superhero name is Mrs. Incredible, or Elastigirl, is a fictional character created for the 2004 animated film *The Incredibles* produced by Pixar.

Introduction: Changing Worlds of Work

Imagine

Imagine a job that takes you places you have never been before. A job that invites you to meet interesting, new people. A job beyond the monotony and drudgery of doing the same thing over and over again. That offers you freedom and flexibility. This is what temporary, flexible work in its imaginary version may be like, or what it promises to be. Now, imagine a job that requires you to move around according to the demands of your employer, where you never really have time to get to know your workmates, where the pay level is uncertain and the future as well. You are expected to bend and adapt to the shifting demands of the client and the job at hand. This is another version of temporary, flexible work. Neither of these versions is truer than the other. There are as many worlds of work as there are temporary employees. Almost.

Even so, this does not mean that there are no patterns to be seen, no structures to reveal, or no larger pictures to be drawn. Indeed, there are regularities within temporary, flexible work, even if they tend to be blurred in the high-flying rhetoric of free agents, dynamic markets, and entrepreneurship.

Temporary, flexible work is set within a particular articulation of global capitalism, post-Fordism, and new regulatory systems. True, these articulations show a great degree of local variation and have their own particular expressions. However, contemporary flexible work, in all its facets, expresses the juncture points of particular ideas and ideologies of work and production systems, of organizational fads and fashions; and of the regulatory set-up of labour markets.

Work occupies a central place in people's lives. It provides us not only with a means of subsistence, but also with a sense of identity and community (Miller and Rose 1995, Noon and Blyton 1997). So also with temporary and flexible work. Advancement within work, conceptualized as 'career', provides a point of reference and meaning for the individual, and works to integrate, tie closer, as well as distinguish and separate workmates from one another. As local economies become more tied into global financial flows, as organizational structures are transformed in line with new templates, and labour markets are re-regulated, our relations to work change as well. Concomitantly, so do ways of constructing career and community from within the realms of work. In a general sense, work may not be the great shaper of identities it once used to be in western industrialized nations, but one among many sources for identification and community. Especially when work is less tied to place and particular groups of people, and more fluid in relation to place and time, we see a differentiation of ways of relating to work. Even so, the workplace continues to be a pre-eminent site for the making, contestation, and reshaping of human identity, individual and collective (Miller and Rose 1995: 428).

At the heart of the forces of change in global capitalism is 'flexibilization' (Piore and Sabel 1984, Harvey 1989). 'Flexible accumulation' has entailed considerable reorganizations of production systems, markets, financial flows, work patterns and employment contracts. These changes have been taken to epitomize a paradigmatic shift, or a new phase of capitalism, referred to as 'disorganized capitalism', post-Fordism (Lash and Urry 1987, Offe 1985), or the 'new world capitalist order' (Harvey 1989). Even though the effects of these changes penetrate unevenly, and take different trajectories in different places, they have meant greater space for market forces to operate and set their imprints on the everyday work lives of a great number of people across the world. Flexibilization brings to the fore the growing powers of organizational rationalization strategies, including a concentration on core competencies, offshore outsourcing of production to areas where labour comes cheaper, automation and standardization of production systems, dependence on expert knowledge, casualization of work contracts, and the like (see, for example, Pfeffer and Baron 1988). In this sense, flexibilization functions as a key point of reference. Given the translocal distribution of organizations and their employees, organizations can no longer accurately be understood as being delineated by spatial boundaries, but rather by interaction and communication which transcend and cross over the more traditional delineators of organizations, and through their control of resources that flow in global circuits. New kinds of relations between organizations and their employees emerge, as labour markets and organizations are restructured towards higher degrees of flexibility and mobility. This implies a move away from regular long-term employment towards increasing reliance on part-time, temporary or sub-contracted work arrangements. A growing number of people are now employed on non-standard or casual contracts, short-term contracts, zero-hour or in the 'black economy'. Likewise, 'self-employment' and 'independent contracting' are becoming alternatives to regular contracts or to unemployment. Even for regular employees work schedules, contracts and skills are becoming more varied, and more and more jobs are going temporary. Today, client companies can ask for skilled engineers, marketing professionals, sales managers, medical doctors and executives as well as the more traditional categories of administrators, receptionists, secretaries, data entry clerks and warehouse telephone operators. Even services like religious or ethical counselling can be brokered through temporary staffing agencies.

This book engages with the flexibilization of work contracts and how this process feeds into contemporary transformations of career and community. Its focus is the experiences and perspectives of temporary employees themselves and how they make sense of and navigate through competitive labour markets. Whilst there are a number of significant contributions to the understanding of flexibilization from a social science perspective, there are fewer accounts from 'the inside', so to speak. What does this world look like from the inside? What do the 'temps' themselves say about their work lives? How do they construct a sense of career and community in discontinuous work assignments and relations? What does being flexible mean in practice? And what can the move towards flexible work contracts tell us about organizational change in general, and about changing forms of governance and control in particular?

The metaphor of the 'vagabond', in the title of this book, suggested itself because of the trajectories and narratives of temporary employees, which told of translocal motion and of a constant readiness to move. The 'mobility imperative' is the result of global capitalist market forces at play, with organizational structures demanding versatile and skilled employees to meet urgent needs and fill unforeseen vacancies. In the ideal image of the flexible production model, movement is depicted as unproblematic; rather, it is at the organizational level that the impediments exist. Dynamic management models are meant to take care of these hindrances. In the 'how-to' literature for people moving into, or already part of, the flexible workforce, the impediments are to be found in the attitudes towards mobility and change, and in the lack of skills and proficiencies that might exist. Such impediments are to be dealt with at an individual level, by responsible job candidates. Mobility could then be reconceptualized as involving empowerment, self-actualization, and as a learning opportunity.

As we shall see, however, mobility does not come without expectations, demands and controls being placed on the individual. Vagabonding also requires that you learn the tricks of the trade, and how to relate to expectations and demands from those around you. You need to know how to distinguish a 'good' place to stop from a 'bad' one; how to approach the locals so as to establish a relation that will work, temporarily at least; and how to read the map and know the territory. In fact, workplace mobility is fraught with challenges, tensions, and conflicts that are not all that visible in organizational ideals, management models or labour market policies. It is in these zones of tension, in the regulatory gaps and the frictions arising from the very discontinuities of work, that work in the global economy takes shape. These tensions inflect mobility and add limitations to the freedoms that accompany workplace vagabonding.

'Workplace vagabonds', that is, the people who make up the new, emerging worlds of temporary and flexible work, are in this sense pioneers in establishing new ways of relating to work, career and community. As established points of reference, such as the local workplace, the permanent contract and the concept of career, lose their traditional bearings and gain new meanings, employees of the new, emerging world of work find alternative ways of navigating successfully in the labour market. And these ways are themselves fraught with tensions and contradictions.

As an anthropologist, my venture has been to find my feet in the world of flexible, temporary work and to give an account from the perspective of those who work within it. Over the course of five years, I have been in and out of the field, met with, interviewed, and observed 'temps', managers of temporary employment agencies, assignment coordinators, employees at client organizations, union representatives, as well as state agency representatives, in Sweden, Great Britain and the US. Although my informants represent a handful of different temporary services, I have chosen to trace the experiences of temps more specifically through Olsten Corporation, a US-based, transnational provider of temporary staffing services worldwide.[1] Lots of conversations, discussions and events have unfolded. And lots of ideas have been born, tried out, some abandoned, some kept. The fragmented nature of flexible work has remained a strong experience, and one I try to convey, but I have also had it on my agenda to ferret out the big picture, and to grasp at the interconnections, dependencies and frictions. One way to combine these experiences of fragmentation and discontinuity, on the one hand, and interconnectedness and continuity, on the other, has been to position flexible, temporary jobs at the interface of an array of forces, between different expectations and aspirations, between different organizations, systems of control, and between work and market. The ethnographic perspective reveals specific alignments of market rationality, post-Fordist modes of organization, and notions of agency and responsibility, that together constitute a particular space for flexible, temporary work and its governance.

Temporary work in itself is nothing new, but the particularities of contemporary flexible work have to do with particular articulations of aspirations and control systems, and in this sense, its 'newness' merits some recognition and consideration.

The temporary employees in this study are people employed through temporary staffing agencies. In relation to employment contracts, 'flexibility' is understood to mean work arrangements other than full-time, permanent contracts. Here, my focus is set on a more limited category in the flexible workforce: employees who are involved in what is loosely referred to as 'agency work'. Workers have contracts of paid employment from one organization, that is, the agency, but typically work at the site of and/or under instructions from a second organization which pays the agency a fee for their services. This means that the temporary employment agency places the employee on short-term contracts, during which he, or more commonly she, is assigned to work for and under the control of the undertaking or establishment making use of his or her services. Thus, the locus of work is a key differentiating feature of temporary help work.

Within a context of transforming organizational structures, the book explores the ways in which 'workplace vagabonds' go about constructing career and community under changing and discontinuous conditions.[2] The book is based on around one hundred interviews and some degree of participant observation with temporary agency workers and staff at Olsten Corporation (now Adecco) in Sweden, the UK and the US, over a number of years in the late 1990s.[3] Interviews have also been conducted with labour market experts in the European Commission, trade union representatives, and representatives of branch organizations. As part of the research process, temporary staffing agency internal documents, such as policy documents, information leaflets, administrative forms and promotional material, have also been studied. The temporary employees whose worklives and experiences are the subject of this book are mostly engaged in clerical work, that is, they work as administrative assistants, receptionists, switchboard operators, marketing assistants, financial assistants, and the like. A majority of them are women ranging in age from nineteen to fifty.

In Bauman's terminology (1995: 94), the vagabond is also a stranger. He or she can never be the inborn, the resident, the one with his roots solidly in the ground, but the vagabond often dreams of just that – just as the 'temp' often dreams of a regular employment contract later on. 'Everywhere he goes he is *in*, but nowhere *of* the place,' Bauman says, with reference to Georg Simmel's classic essay on the stranger (Simmel 1950). This simultaneous presence and absence also characterizes the social situation of temps. It has also been noticed by the industry leaders. The chief executive of one of the largest Swedish temporary staffing agencies told me that when taking in new temporary employees, they look for 'lone wolves with social competence'. 'We need people who can be relied on wherever they're thrown in, to do a good job and to fit in. But they also have to be able to keep their distance, to represent the agency in a professional manner'.

Temporary agency employment is a category that constitutes a small proportion of the labour force, but one that is growing in importance and numbers on a global scale. By no means does this pragmatic definition exhaust the variety of flexible employees in contemporary labour markets. But temporary agency work provides particular empirical material 'to think with'; one that is suitable for the variety of ways in which its actors continuously challenge established organizational boundary-lines. Although the material upon which this book is based concerns temporary help workers, I believe that with the growing share of temporary, contract, and contingent work arrangements, the experiences and arguments may well serve to illuminate certain aspects of the contemporary world of work more broadly.

Outline of the book

The configuration of work, capitalism and agency constitutes what Paul Rabinow (2003) has referred to as an 'anthropological problem'. In the growing scope and scale of market ideology and practice, it is important to examine how new practices of work, new ideas about agency, and new normative vocabularies emerge and become institutionalized. We should ask where the organizational templates and the cognitive maps provided for workers originate and how they are diffused, negotiated and contested. Not least, we need to enquire into what these configurations of power mean for human beings, individually and collectively. In their complexity, they constitute appropriate crossroads for reflection on and invigoration of anthropology's potential contribution today, in relation to the tools, perspectives and claims that can be made about contemporary market culture. In Rabinow's words, 'we are currently undergoing and participating in a distinctive set of inflections about labor, life, and language' (2005: 41). Yet, there exists little in the way of unifying knowledge about this inflection. All the more urgent, therefore, to 'problematize', in the Foucauldian sense, to place oneself observingly, questioningly and reflexively in the midst of contending systems of knowledge and claims about the nature of flexible work today.

This book engages with changes in labour markets towards more flexible work contracts and the reordering of relations and responsibilities between actors. The move towards a more flexible labour market involves changes in the ways people and organizations are to be understood as well as changes in assumptions regarding subjectivity, agency and responsibility and the type of knowledge and competences that are valued in companies, employment agencies and among policy makers. Such transformations are indicative of important shifts in the nature of economy and polity, and they signify changes in culture and ideology. By taking a closer look at the world of flexible labour, and how the imaginings and preferences of flexible workers interact with organizational requests, we may move towards a clearer understanding of larger trends regarding perspectives on work, career and work community.

Some of the larger trends that influence flexible, temporary employment work are discussed in the first chapter of this book. The context of my research into 'temping' is one of large-scale social and work transformation – of the globalization of social relations and organizational forms, of economic interdependencies and neoliberal cultural change programmes. The globalization of work and the changing forms of labour market regulation have significant impacts on the context of our daily rounds of work, and eventually on how we perceive work, career and subjectivity. It is at the very crossroads of such influences that the particularities of flexible temporary work are articulated.

What draws people into the flexible labour market? Chapter 2 of this book engages with some of the motives that draw people into flexible temporary work and the kinds of imaginings and hopes they carry with them. The flexible labour market attracts people from all walks of life: people looking for an alternative to the breadwinner model, people wanting to learn more, people searching for a permanent, open-ended job. But the temporary employment agency also has its expectations and demands, as do the client organizations to which the temps are assigned to work. From the outset, imaginings, preferences and expectations have to be balanced. The temping field is also one that poses a number of challenges for the anthropologist looking for context, continuous relations, and a field that can be located in time and place. I will reflect on how I myself entered the temping field as a researcher, and how I tried to find my way into the discontinuous and translocal field of temping. Chapter 3 targets the mobility imperative that comes with temporary agency work and the normative requests and adaptations that this entails. Being on the move, crossing organizational boundaries, is an important aspect of temping worklife and has to be learnt. The patterns of mobility of temps are deeply entangled with globalized labour markets, yet they can seldom direct their own yo-yo movements, as it were. In Chapter 4, I will focus on the temporal aspect of temping, which is intrinsically linked with the spatial characteristics. Temporary employees also have to deal with the transient character of their employment and the risks attached to it. Being prepared, embracing change, and learning to make use of 'time tools' are part of constructing a sense of continuity in the midst of contingency. By now, we will see that temping is largely about acquiring a transferable set of skills, and a transferable self, that can be relied upon in changing contexts. The constant readiness required of those who undertake flexible, temporary work also involves collaborating in continuous evaluations by both agency and client organization. This evaluative gaze is a constant companion of temporary employees, and one that also engages the temp herself or himself through expectations that one takes on responsibility for one's own career and development. Here, we will take a look at how the employees are evaluated and rewarded as 'good' temps, and how flexibility is fostered and rewarded. In transient and mobile forms of work, where colleagues are often mixed up with competitors and clients, what happens to the sense of work community? The challenges of establishing such collegial relations and a sense of community are discussed in Chapter 6. This chapter will also reflect on the position of temps as 'betwixt and between' the normal coordinates of time and space in worklife, and what this position may mean for their relations with colleagues and their sense of identity. In the last chapter, I will allow myself some reflections on contemporary worklife in the light of my experiences from the temping business. Flexible worklife, I suggest, speaks of changes in contemporary culture and social life. A competitive culture is being fostered, in which we learn to reckon with market forces as points of reference for the crafting of our mental images and our actions. While we are taught to see ourselves more and more as individual performers we are at the same time drawn into wider circuits of change that we may not be able to control or even see clearly, at all times. The interplay of the larger forces of a globalizing capitalism and of concomitant organizational change should not lead us to turn a blind eye to the implications they might have for our forms of togetherness, or for ourselves. It is in this crossfire that we stand today.

1
Work in the Global Economy

Working through the prism of globalization

In a volume on the significance of the cultural study of work, Harper and Lawson (2003: p. xvi) state: 'There is no greater issue in the current configuration of work than globalization.' Without doubt, globalization is a force to be reckoned with in the world of work. Economic relations are becoming increasingly globalized and the mobility of finance capitalism challenges the capacity of nation states to control market actors through political action. Labour markets, too, are more tightly connected to each other across nation states. Globalization moves jobs such as software development, customer services and assembly work to different places in the world depending on proficiency, wage levels and production costs. In the search for new markets and profitable production arrangements, business organizations are outsourcing and externalizing their operations across great distances. Such organizations challenge established boundaries – spatial, organizational and cultural – and contribute to the web of global interconnectedness. They play a vital role in organizing people, ideas and products, and contribute to restructuring and transforming the experience of work for a large proportion of the workforce.[1]

The global market redistributes work opportunities, rewards and risks along new axes. For the well-educated and skilled, the people with recognized credentials, globalization opens up new spaces and avenues for pursuing exciting and rewarding job opportunities. In the telecommunications industry, computing, finance and the academic world, many professionals have agendas with lots of mobility written into them, and are able to take advantage of the many benefits out there. Accordingly, we may now perceive work as being increasingly translocal in character. The world of work is now populated by large numbers of moving groups of people whose skills can be put to use in a variety of different organizational contexts without losing much of its value; such people are sometimes labelled 'cosmopolitans' (Hannerz 1990), 'symbolic analysts' (Reich 1992) or 'portfolio workers' (see, for example, Cohen and Mallon 1999)'. For these groups of people, skills, knowledge and ideas are becoming increasingly de-territorialized, allowing for greater degrees of freedom to carry their professional portfolio along to different contexts. Work has lost much of its spatial bearings. The continuous movement, and the concomitant revaluation of space, is a key characteristic of large numbers of people in globalizing and restructuring organizations – consultants, businessmen and temporaries alike.

But alongside the enhanced global and mobile character of business, information and capital flows, other social spheres are being increasingly localized, or fixed to set patterns of mobility. Whilst flexibility of work conditions as well as mobility may be voluntary and chosen by some categories of people – those who enjoy the privileges of high-status knowledge and position – there are large groups of people who remain fixed to particular jobs and workplaces, and for whom ever-more sophisticated systems of production and technology mean little or nothing at all. To a large extent, the increased freedom of movement for some professional groups relies on more spatially stable groups of workers for its maintenance.

Outsourcing of production and services is one way in which organizational mobility is written into globalized patterns, whilst simultaneously circumscribing the mobility of some groups of people. In a recent volume, Aihwa Ong (2006: 158) describes outsourcing as opening up a new kind of Asian-American nexus in knowledge work: outsourcing may be conceptualized as a form of the 'immutable mobile', ie Bruno Latour's term for global forms that have 'properties of being mobile but also *immutable, presentable, readable,* and *combinable* with one another' (italics in original). Here, the immutable market rationality of efficiency, codes, and protocols is drawn together with mobile knowledge and skills, an interaction that changes the claims of identity and citizenship, Ong argues. As corporations seek lower costs for knowledge workers, entitlements become delinked from citizenship and relinked to the mobile economic and cultural skills in global circuits.

'Labor arbitrage', understood as the practice of buying low in a market and selling high elsewhere, Ong continues, exposes people to the fluctuations of the global market, and shifts well-paying jobs across borders. 'Labor arbitrage is the latest technique for exploiting time-space coordinates in order to accumulate profits, putting into play a new kind of flexibility that makes the American worker ineligible in some high-tech domains' (Ong 2006: 174).

Moreover, novel varieties of 'body shopping', as a system of labour contracting that relocates cheaper skilled labour in the high-wage, high-tech market, has gradually gained hold in dynamic regions of innovation and in labour markets with an abundance of high-skilled workers. In a recent study of the IT labour market in southern India and Australia, Xiang Biao (2007) shows how the industry's flexible labour market system works by recruiting IT workers in different countries through 'body-shopping' practices. In this practice, recruited workers are farmed out to clients as project-based labour, and upon a project's completion either placed with a different client, or 'benched' to await the next placement. In this way, labour is managed globally to serve volatile market fluctuation and capital movement. Biao argues that underpinning this practice of global body shopping are unequal socioeconomic relations on multiple levels, in which it is the benched workers who, in their everyday realities, have to sustain the flexibility of abstract financial movement and accumulation.

Furthermore, the significance of mobility in a globalizing labour market is evidenced in the rigour with which governments are attempting not only to facilitate, but to control, the movements of people across state borders. While some categories of workers are seen to be wanted and welcomed across borders, others are being restrained in their movements, and new kinds of regulations are being invented to prevent them from 'invading' nation states. The current European Union and national debates on the pros and cons of allowing migrant workers to move more freely across national boundaries is evidence of this economic and political dilemma. A great deal of time and energy is spent on regulating who is to be able to move freely about, and who is restrained in doing so.

The deterritorialization of work thus sets up new lines of cleavage. Some groups of workers stand a weak chance of ever deciding on their own patterns of mobility, but are caught in webs spun by their more mobile contemporaries (see, for example, Nyberg Sörensen and Fog Olvig 2002). Voluntary mobility, not mobility as such, has come to signify a sense of freedom and agency, and has become one the most celebrated values in the globalized labour market. Globalization, then, provides new incentives to study work and work cultures, to understand how these are affected by, and contribute to, the mobilities of capital and of ideas.

Flexibilizing work and employment

'Flexibility' is the *modus operandi* of global capitalism today. It influences significantly work and employment in the new global economy. One may argue that flexibility lies at the very heart of the forces connected to the workings of global capitalism. 'Flexible accumulation' has meant substantial reorganizations of production systems, finance flows, work organization and employment contracts at transnational levels. What has been referred to as 'post-Fordism', 'disorganized capitalism', or the 'new world capitalist order' involves a flexibilization of production and labour. In broad terms, with the time-space compression involved in globalization, the development of information technology, the reliance on information and knowledge more generally, and new forms of networking and mobility, the trope of flexibilization has swept across the world of organizations.

We may note here, that the trope of flexibility does not stop at the doorstep of work and organization, however, but filters more generally through contemporary society and culture. It suggests a new configuration of rights and obligations in relation to citizenship and democracy (Ong 1999). The value of 'being flexible' is promoted in social life through notions such as 'social competence'; in education, by the focus on 'flexible learning' and 'lifelong learning'; in our emotional spheres, through ideas of 'emotional intelligence'; in medicine and immunology (see Martin 1994); evidently so in fitness training, with its idealized image of the human body as versatile, agile and resilient; and also in the self-improvement or 'make-over' culture (see McGee 2005). The trope of flexibility thus stretches beyond organization and work to provide a sense of direction for human beings in different spheres of contemporary life.

Exactly what this new type of flexibilization means, however, is an issue that continues to be debated. In relation to the labour market, flexibility entails 'the ability to change or react to change with little penalty in time, effort, cost or performance' (Benner 2002: 14). Although the firm has generally been the unit of analysis, this applies as well to networks of organizations, and to individuals. There are, as well, varieties of flexibility, such as 'numerical' or 'external', 'functional' or 'internal', 'temporal', and the like.[2] For my purposes, I find Benner's distinction between 'flexible work' and 'flexible employment' useful: first, because it escapes the notion of a distinction between core–periphery workforces so often implied in an analysis of flexible labour markets; second, because it draws a distinction between the flexibility that resides in the employment contract on the one hand and the inflexibility of work processes on the other. In this volume, I depart from an interest in what the flexibilization of employment does to the experiences of individual temps, with analytical emphasis on the latter rather than on the small print of the employment contract itself.

In the globalized landscape of work, a distinctively new vocabulary and set of buzzwords have thus gained salience, both as organizing metaphors and policy instruments. 'Flexibility', and with it terms such as 'employability', 'lifelong learning' and 'entrepreneurship', are placed at the centre of attention. Recruitment ads, employment agency documents and corporate policy, as well as the policy recommendations of intergovernmental organizations, underline the significance of tuning in to these demands. Competence and skill are seen as perishable goods, of strategic value to individuals as well as organizations and even nations. Knowledge, ideas and intellectual capacity are now the hard currency in increasingly competitive labour markets. Flexibility offers to free us from the 'rigidities of the labour market' so feared by economists, and to open up more dynamic and agile forms of work arrangements. Flexible organizations provide a model of freedom for individuals, quite unlike the experiences of static and fixed bureaucracies that Max Weber called 'iron cage'.

With regard to work and labour markets, 'employability' is a steady companion of flexibility (see Garsten and Jacobsson 2004). It suggests the capacity and agency of individuals to create their own job opportunities and careers, not having to wait passively for the welfare state to provide the opportunities. In a similar way, 'entrepreneurship' and 'lifelong learning', pushed by large-scale organizations such as the EU and the OECD, are saturated with the positive connotations of self-development, skills refinement, professional development, and a general broadening and deepening of knowledge, and indicate the emphasis placed on readiness for change and learning-to-learn anew in the competitive global labour market (see Weinert et al. 2001). Fluid and polyvalent buzzwords such as these nevertheless offer a sense of direction to what might otherwise be experienced as the opportunistic and chance-like movements of contemporary capitalism.

Most importantly, this vocabulary tells of a transition from relatively stable patterns of work to more uncertain structural arrangements, with new demands being placed on the individual. A central tenet is that getting a job is to a large degree dependent upon the power of initiative of the individual, upon one's own sense of responsibility for one's actions and decisions. This conceptual topography prescribes a changed and arguably more limited role for the state, greater space for market forces to operate, and, not least, greater pressure – and responsibilities – on the individual. Aspirations and expectations are no longer judged against the norm and ideal of permanent, lifelong work, but against a set of opportunities and risks. Ultimately, this development has important implications for the way relations and contracts between employees and employers, unions and corporations, and politics and market forces are to be designed, and hence, for power relations (Stråth 2000, Garsten and Jacobsson 2004). With a view to market demand and fluctuation, contracts can legitimately be made to adjust more tightly to the core organizational business and to immediate needs. Contracts are subject to change, as it were, according to a short-term market logic that is difficult to question.

In many instances though, flexibility denies exactly that which it promises. To implement labour market flexibility in the economic sense, that is, to dismantle work contract regulations and social protections and lower levels of taxation, the agility and versatility of the employee needs to be framed and made responsive to that of the corporation and of capital. More often than not, it is the employee who has to meet the standards of flexibility set for him or her by the employer and by those in command of resources. The freedom of an individual to choose, to accept or refuse an assignment, to set his or her own rules for the game, is most often constrained by the suppliers of work opportunities and contracts. Flexibility is thus not an unbounded landscape of possibilities, but a bounded space of openings and closures in which individuals have to navigate as best they can. Paradoxically then, the supplier bias of flexibility induces a certain degree of inflexibility and rigidity to work practices (see Bauman 1998a, Chapter 5).

Concepts such as flexibility, employability, entrepreneurship and lifelong learning tend to mask their social, relational character. But flexibility can only be understood in relation to something or someone else (Bauman 1998a: 104). The concept postulates versatility on the part of one in relation to the other. In the best of circumstances, this versatility is mutual. More often, however, it involves an unbalanced relation in which the capacity to bend is expected from one party, while the other decides on the premises. Hence, flexibility involves a redistribution of power and agency. In the labour market, flexibility is promised on the demand side, as it were, as offering new opportunities for workers, while it is more often practised on the supply side, that is, by those offering the job opportunities.

From a critical, welfare-centred perspective, the changing of destinations and workplaces is more often connected to the idea of an increasing marginalization of the workforce. The flexibility associated with temporary work is regarded as a sign of powerlessness, of work on demand, and of a lower rung on the status ladder. More market-oriented perspectives view mobility as liberating, empowering, and a source of dynamism and development for the individual employee as well as for the labour market at large. Instead of a marginalized and dependent job-seeker, actors are posited as 'free agents', capable of finding their own ways across the shifting landscape of opportunities (see, for example, Pink 2001).

The consequences of flexible employment and flexible work have been studied by several scholars, who have contributed complementary understandings to the changing worlds of work.[3] Among the more recent ones I would like to mention here Stephen Barley and Gideon Kunda's (2004) ethnography of 'itinerant professionals', that is, temporary professionals in the information technology sector. The authors take a close look at how the business operates from the perspectives of those who do the actual work, the clients who employ them, the regular employees who work alongside them, and the staffing agencies who broker them. From within the context of vibrant Silicon Valley, they show how the flexibility of the knowledge economy often differs from its promise, and how it involves living the tension between professionalism on the one hand and adapting to the requirements of the work context on the other.

Carla Freeman's (2000) ethnography of Barbadian 'pink-collar workers' on the global assembly lines of information work provides an insightful contribution to our understanding of the complex relationships between gender, social class and culture. Freeman argues convincingly that 'the forces with which the social order and multinational corporate power maintain legitimacy in the Barbadian context of the informatics industry involve not only capitalist discipline but also the flexibility on the part of corporations and the state to heed women's interests that are grounded in their particular, gendered, Afro-Caribbean, late-twentieth-century culture' (2000: 28). One of the major contributions of this book, in my opinion, is that it reveals the 'gendering' embedded in capitalist production, and how gender, as socially imputed meanings associated with maleness and femaleness, is 'made' among flexible, female workers along the global assembly line, and how the market, in the way of consumption as well as labour, enters into the process.

With Rose (1999: 156–158), we may contend that flexibilization has both a 'macro-economic' and a 'micro-economic' moment. While the macro-economic directs attention to the flexible arrangement of labour as an explicitly political strategy of economic government, the micro-economic moment addresses struggles over the appropriate tactics to increase the flexibility of relations between the individual and the workplace. This book treats temporary agency work as a disciplinary space where the economic, the social and the subjective are brought together in the making of flexible employees. Flexible, temporary work, in my view is the key junction point between the forces of global organizational restructurings, market-driven employment relations and subjective identity formation. The story departs from within one transnational, American corporation, and traces the imaginings and trajectories of temps across organizational boundaries. What it wishes to convey is an understanding of how life in the 'temping zone' is worked out in between organizational claims to control and governance and people's strivings to create a sense of continuity and direction out of mobile and transient work relations.

Mediating flexible jobs: Olsten Corporation

With increased flexiblization of employment contracts, the role of intermediaries in mediating between workers and employers in the process of job matching and brokering employment relationships have increased significantly (see, for example, Benner 2002). Private intermediaries, such as temporary help agencies, cater to a need for adapting to rapid change in staffing, in work requirements and organization of production. The staffing industry has since the mid-twentieth century evolved from providing mostly unskilled work in the industrial sector or short-term replacements for sick or temporarily absent workers to placing more skilled workers on a more regular basis. Over time, they have abandoned their nickname 'temp firms' in favour of 'staffing firms', indicating the broadening of their activities to provide firms with staffing solutions more generally, including permanent placement, payroll, outplacement, and other managed services (Kedia and Tufano 2001: 2).

The temporary staffing business is dominated by large transnational corporations, such as Adecco, Manpower and Randstad, who employ millions of workers all across the world. These corporations are in command of formidable resources: manpower and financial assets, as well as informational resources, and their influence on local and translocal labour markets should not be underestimated. They also have their own particular policies and practices for running their business which are diffused across the countries in which they operate. There is reason to speak here not only of 'globalization' in a general sense, but of a spread of corporate values and norms that can be pinned down more clearly to the cultural roots of their respective organizations. Managerial techniques, vocabularies and priorities are largely streamlined across locations, albeit with some degree of appropriate 'localization' to allow for the 'social assets' coupled with the sharing of local and tacit knowledge, informal rules and norms, and cultural specificities.

At the time of my fieldwork, the company in focus went under the name of Olsten Corporation, with its headquarters in Melville, Long

Island, in the state of New York. Olsten had been founded in 1950 by William Olsten, who was reported as having placed his wife and sister as the firm's first temps. The firm grew rapidly, with a focus on health care and staffing services, and went public in 1967. By 1998, the company was the third-largest staffing company in the world, with a market share of 3.9 percent, operating in 14 countries with 1,500 offices. Its regional office in Santa Clara, California, was one of the more important temporary help nodes in the area, with crucial connections to the sprawling computing and high-tech business in the Silicon Valley area. From the modest location and exterior of its office premises, one of the thousands of greyish low buildings throughout the Valley, its significance could rarely have been guessed.

Olsten also aggressively expanded its business outside the US. Through a series of acquisitions from 1994 to 1997 it substantially increased its presence in Europe and Latin America. Two of the companies acquired by Olsten, or in which Olsten purchased majority stakes, were Sweden's by-then third-largest staffing firm, Kontorsjouren, and Office Angels in the UK, one of the biggest players in the UK recruitment and staffing market. For my research, serendipity truly played a role here, since my original contacts with temping firms in Sweden and the UK respectively had been with Kontorsjouren and Office Angels – as independent companies. I now found myself in a privileged position in which to trace the transnational connections between different locations in one and the same company. The transnational harmonization was visible in management systems, in culture, as well as in the physical layout of office premises. The American, east-coast headquarters were in this sense made present and visible in distant locations.

Following a lagging performance in the staffing industry and a sharp decline in stock price, Olsten's staffing business was acquired by Adecco in 2000.[4] At this time, I had completed my empirical research and followed the company from a distance. Adecco had been formed in 1996 from the merger of Swiss Adia SA with the French firm Ecco. The Swiss-based Adecco had since grown rapidly and was by 1999 the world's largest staffing company. The staffing business of Adecco complemented Adecco's business in the US and in the rest of the world nicely. Olsten's prominent presence in the IT business would also allow Adecco to increase its market share in this segment. Also, Adecco management felt that the cultures of the two companies were compatible, which made Olsten a desirable acquisition. At present, Adecco claims to be 'the world leader in human resource solutions, with a comprehensive service offering that includes temporary and contract staffing, outsourcing, permanent recruitment, outplacement and career services, training and consulting' (www.adecco.com, visited 18 June 2007). With 6,700 offices in 70 countries, the company is a transnational private job intermediary of substantial scale and influence. In the following account I will speak about the company as Olsten in general and Office Angels when referring specifically to the UK subsidiary (which kept its name), since that is how I knew them during my fieldwork period.

Transnational trends and shifting regulatory contexts

Olsten, like other transnational staffing agencies, has also to adjust to the national legislative and cultural context in which they are localized. To understand the workings of flexible, temporary employment requires an appreciation of differing historical and national trajectories as well as sensitivity to the standardizing effects of transnational operations. Here, I will provide a broad sweep of the differing national contexts in which the Olsten temps work.

In Sweden, how and by whom employment issues should be regulated has always been a central concern (see, for example, Furåker 1979). Since the 1940s, the State took more or less full control over permanent and temporary employment placement, and private employment agencies were gradually abolished. The centralization of job allocation into the hands of State agencies was an important step in the realization of the Swedish welfare state. In this ideological context, regular, salaried employment functioned as an ideological tool and cornerstone. The Labour Market Board exercised control over the observance of the law and could grant permission to run placement bureaus for profit (SOU 1997: 58). Swedish governments have since stressed a strong commitment to full and permanent employment, accompanied by direct state intervention and responsibility. Entrusting these issues to the care of the State was to ensure that market forces and private interests did not intervene in the process in search of profit and private gain. The legislation of the temping industry in large part built on the ILO conventions regulating job placement for profit.

However, increasing global competition, deregulation of financial markets and pressure to create more dynamic organizational structures, along with uncertainties regarding the exact interpretation of labour market regulations, paved the way for the growth of private temporary employment agencies during the 1970s and afterwards. There was, especially in some segments of the industry, a strong need for administrative personnel who could temporarily relieve corporations of pressure during peak production periods and externalize employment risk. The temping business thus continued to grow, in spite of relatively strict regulation. Occasional State inspections and sanctions did not put a halt to its growth. On the contrary, it continued to prosper in the margins of State legislative structures, apparently awaiting progressive deregulation.

Since the early 1990s, concomitant with and sustained by exceptionally high levels of unemployment, there has been a deregulation of the Swedish labour market. The ILO's Convention 96, which had prohibited profit-driven private placement, was also abandoned. A new law in 1992 meant that temporary placement of employees, with some restrictions, was legalized, with no requirements for authorization by State agencies. In 1993, another law was passed, bringing about the deregulation of the existing State monopoly on permanent placement and the abolition of the restrictions on temporary placement that still operated. These regulatory changes dramatically changed the scene. They signalled an opening for private firms to recruit and lease workforces for profit as well as for transnational staffing agencies to start operations in Sweden.[5] Temporary employment agencies now had the freedom to expand. Even so, the government continued to play an important role in the regulation of temporary agency work through its surveillance and sanctions, thereby keeping flexibility at bay.[6]

The transformation of the Swedish labour market towards temporary staffing speaks of regulatory changes unseen for half a century, with responsibilities being recast under the headings of deregulation and flexibilization. State agencies are now responding to the penetration of market values into the labour market. Whereas labour unions, employers' associations and corporate leaders may, and indeed do, have differing views on what exactly flexibilization should mean, there is a general agreement around the idea that the labour market actors need to embrace mobility and entrepreneurship in order to boost business and counteract unemployment. This involves the flexibilization of employment contracts, flexible work organization, and flexible working hours. The latter connects with, and is dressed in the language of, a continuous concern for the quality of working life, placing primary stress on flexibility *for* workers, not *of* workers. Flexible hours are seen as an important part of a more democratic, productive and fulfilling mode of governing work, compatible with a more expanded notion of the role of the worker. They are generally regarded as promoting women's participation in the labour market, whereas flexible and contingent contracts are generally viewed as threatening gender equality.

However, it is around the issue of flexible employment contracts that the public debate has been most intense. Against the established background of a strong State framework of governance and control, and of full and permanent employment as the norm, flexible contracts constitute a powerful threat. Accordingly, temporary agency workers were long referred to statistically as 'atypical' or classified as 'unemployed'. Not least, their existence stirred political debates about the marginalization of certain groups, notably less well-educated women. Temporary agency workers were seen to be at risk financially as well as missing out on professional development and career.

In the 1990s, a Commission on Working Life Issues was established, with the explicit aim of investigating how the labour market could be made more flexible, while maintaining a degree of security for employees. A special investigation was also organized on behalf of the Labour Department with the aim of analysing the effects and consequences of the deregulation. In relation to the temporary employment industry, one goal was to look into eventual need for new regulation and a mandatory State authorization of private temporary employment agencies. The conclusion, which was made public in the spring of 1998, was that no further legislative regulation or State authorization was needed, a decision applauded by the industry but provoking negative reactions from labour unions. For the temporary placement industry, this signalled acceptance of their business by the State, and the legitimization of further growth and a general move towards flexible employment contracts. Neoliberal market rhetoric about economic growth, downsizing and outsourcing thus combined with governmental hopes that these moves would also create more job opportunities and ameliorate unemployment statistics.

The legacy of Swedish employment security is reflected in the working conditions of employees in the temporary staffing sector. Temporary work in Sweden is, generally speaking and despite recent changes, relatively clearly regulated by statutory law and collective agreements. Temps are usually employed at agencies on open-ended employment contracts, with a guaranteed salary of at least 80 per cent of the full-time salary. Other benefits, such as health insurance, pension rights and compensation during parental leave, are generally the same as for employees on regular employment contracts. Sector-based collective agreements regarding pay and general conditions exist for most areas. Consequently, average turnover time is higher than for many other European countries: approximately 38 months in the administrative sector and 12 months across sectors.[7] There are also other, less permanent contracts, designed to meet occasional demand. Even so, while employment risk is being increasingly individualized, there is still a relative measure of security for individual temporary agency workers.

Such collective agreements did not come about without effort, however. They were the result of prolonged and heated discussions between unions and employers, in which the Salaried Employees' Union, HTF, played a significant role in pushing the discussions forward. Unions have also been pressing for the right of employees to use working time for educational purposes.[8] Continuous learning is a necessity in this competitive labour market, and temps are regularly reminded by agency staff of the need to upgrade their skills and take tests so as to check out their progress on, for example, using software. However to date, most of this upskilling has taken place outside office hours.

The relation of the staffing sector to the public employment centres in Sweden has also changed from one of mutual mistrust and competition to one characterized by relatively close co-operation. For the employment centres, the staffing agencies are important partners. While the most 'employable' individuals often find their own routes to employment, the more vulnerable job seekers rely on employment centres to assist them. For the staffing agencies, the employment centres perform vital functions in finding potential job candidates, informing people about work in the temporary staffing sector, and the like.

At present, approximately one per cent of the Swedish workforce works through temp agencies (CIETT 2005). As a comparison, the European Union ratio is somewhat higher than two per cent of the workforce (CIETT 2005). According to a report by the European Foundation for Improvement of Living and Working Conditions (2006), approximately sixty per cent of temp workers in Sweden are women. Most of the temporary agency workers are relatively young, with 59 per cent being under 35 years of age. The report also shows that employment in the service sector dominates strongly, with almost seventy-five per cent of jobs in this sector. There is also a tendency towards increased professionalization of the business, convergent with its development in many other countries, including the US. It may be interesting to note here that the educational level of temporary workers in Sweden is somewhat higher than the workforce average. Forty-eight per cent have completed upper secondary school, while 37 per cent have a post-upper secondary school education. The equivalent numbers for the workforce as a whole are 50 and 29 per cent (Fridén et al. 2000: 61).

Whereas the tendencies towards deregulation of the Swedish labour market strikes many as embracing flexibility to a large extent, it is in the UK that the greater resonance of such changes can be discerned (see Allen and Henry 1996: 68). The national institutional configurations and the social norms and practices which underpinned post-war economic expansion have also been progressively undermined, and have given way to a period of experimentation in different organizational forms and different employment and management practices (Walsh 1997: 3). Successive Conservative governments between 1979 and 1997 sought to deregulate the labour market in an attempt to allow employers to operate more freely. Deregulating employment has generally had the effect of shifting the balance away from employment protection towards employment flexibility, involving consequences both for those in work and those out of work, and imposing restrictions on the operations of trade unions (Noon and Blyton 1997: 15–16). This policy of deregulation has been underpinned by theories of neo-classical economics, which hold that economic revival is dependent on allowing market forces to operate free of government intervention and 'artificial' constraints. Outsourcing, subcontracting, and the proliferation of individualized employment, are viewed as demonstrating flexible responses to market demand.

In this process, a new set of political ideals has been articulated, which points to what is perceived as a neglect of the values of autonomy, entrepreneurship and self-motivation. The British debate on 'enterprise culture' connected the notion of flexibility with a distinct set of ideals concerning production and the identity of the worker that aligned ideals of individualism to neoliberal political visions. 'Enterprise' came to mean not simply an organizational form, but a certain mode of activity that could be applied equally to organizations, to individuals within organizations, and to persons in their everyday existence (du Gay 1991, Miller and Rose 1995: 455). The political vocabulary of enterprise, as it took shape in the Thatcherite 1980s, promised a new identity for the individual and gave rise to new strategies of governing the workplace. According to these new ideals, order was to be achieved through individuals improving and disciplining themselves, to become entrepreneurial, flexible, employable and self-sufficient members of society. As Miller and Rose put it: 'The political vocabulary of enterprise established a versatile set of relations among a critique of contemporary institutional forms, a program for the revitalisation of economic life and national power, and an ethics of the self' (1995: 454).

For management doctrines as well as political visions, the new political salience of flexibility and enterprise opened a fertile territory for the development of a variety of change programmes and a series of deregulatory measures aimed at reinvigorating individual initiative and infusing vitality into the labour market. This avenue has also to a large extent been followed by the New Labour Government, which has stressed the importance of reducing 'rigidities' and promoting flexibility in labour markets. Critical voices have aired concern about the 'social dumping' effect of flexibilization as well as its relation to the 'feminization' of work, involving an increased number of women on contingent contracts, but also the infusion of values and manners culturally ascribed to females and thus held to be 'feminine'.[9]

Temporary employment agencies play a vital part in the British flexibilization scenario, as temporary workers are becoming an increasingly significant part of employment planning in Britain. Market reports indicate that the recruitment of temporary workers through temporary employment agencies is increasing annually at a steady pace. At present, an estimated five per cent of the workforce work through employment agencies. The above-mentioned report from the European Foundation for Improvement of Living and Working Conditions (2006) shows that office-based employment still dominates, and service sector jobs are vastly over-represented (86 per cent). The report claims 48 per cent of all temporary agency workers are women, which is a considerably lower percentage than in Sweden. The temporary agency workforce is also very young, 62 per cent being under 30 years of age. In terms of education, the highest qualification achieved is comparable to the employed population overall, but lower than that of other non-permanent employees (Forde 1997).

Whereas the temporary industry in Sweden has gone through a step-by-step deregulation, carefully controlled by the State, it was never heavily regulated in the UK to begin with. In fact, in comparison with the rest of Europe, it stands out as being largely *un*regulated. The UK has never ratified any of the ILO conventions regarding profit-driven job placement. As Hepple (1993: 269) notes, 'It has often been remarked that the approach of United Kingdom Governments unlike those in many other member States has been to allow temporary employment to be market-led, rather than government-led. The organized employment agencies and business have always argued that there is a strong demand for their services and that a State monopoly would be both costly and ineffective.' To speak about deregulation in this context is thus something of a misnomer. Until 1995, however, temporary employment agencies operated on a license from the State, a procedure that is now replaced by an inspection process (SOU 1997: 58). The Employment Agencies Act 1973 and regulations are enforced by the Department of Employment's regional offices, whose officers also have powers to enter the premises of agencies to inspect records and other documents and to obtain information. State intervention in the British labour market has been and continues to be very limited, as is the role of social partners. Collective bargaining in the temping industry has been largely non-existent, even though trade unions have in recent times negotiated agreements, usually regarding individual grievances and with local employment business. Unions have also tried to work for the establishment of the same rights for temporary agency workers as permanent employees, most often on an informal basis. Generally, though, the trend has been towards de-collectivization and non-unionization of the labour market, and of the temporary agency market in particular (see Ackroyd 2007, Pollert 2007). Deregulation, then, has rather involved a reduction in the already restricted scope and extent of statutory employment protection and welfare benefits, the abolition of minimum wage-setting mechanisms and the steady erosion of legal supports for collective bargaining (Walsh 1997: 4).

Despite the steady growth in numbers of temporary workers, they have not been separately identified as a category within British labour law (Hepple 1993: 259). They constitute a wide and diverse category of workers, with a variety of different experiences and needs. The employment relationship statutes are more intricate than those in Sweden (Storrie 2002, Håkansson and Isidorsson 2007). In some cases, the temporary employee is not necessarily considered an 'employee', and the temporary employment agency is not necessarily the 'employer'. Hence, problems often arise as to the character of relations and responsibilities between the parties, and the user may become jointly responsible with the temporary employment agency for the fulfilment of the rights of the temporary agency worker, as in cases where legislative requirements have not been respected (Hepple 1993). Most workers are, nonetheless, taxed and pay social security contributions is if they were dependent employees. However, there is no mutuality of obligation between agency and worker to provide and accept work, and the agency does not in this sense 'control' the work of the temp (Casey 1987: 80).

British practice thus shifts power over the temporary agency worker towards the client organization, whereas in Sweden the employer–employee relation is relatively stronger. British temporary agency workers, as their US colleagues, are consequently free to sign up with several agencies, an option not available in Sweden. Here also, the labelling of the temporary agency worker reflects the differences in the position of the temporary agency worker in the two countries. Whereas in Sweden they are often referred to as 'consultants', stressing their relatively strong position with regard to the employer, in Britain (as well as in the US) they are normally referred to as 'temporaries' or, more commonly, 'temps'. In the following, account 'temp' or 'temporary' will refer to temporary agency workers in Britain, Sweden and the US alike.

Contrary to common belief, regular employment has also long been the norm in the US. The foundations of the American labour market were conceptualized under the New Age Deal after the Great Depression and then institutionalized in labour law and collective bargaining (see, for example, Barley and Kunda 2004: 9–15). In this system, which relied on a bargain struck between employers and employees and which posited reasonable expectations of job security and social benefits, employers had significant obligations to their employees under US law. These obligations did not apply, however, if the employee was an independent contractor, was self-employed, or if he or she had more than one employer, something which often proved to be the case. US employers have been skilled in utilizing this space for manoeuvre, reducing staff 'headcount' by making use of flexible labour.[10]

As in the UK, the temping industry evolved successively from being largely unregulated to become an object of debate and of partial regulation. The general story is that temporary staffing agencies grew as a response to the rapid economic changes and the massive downsizings of the 1990s. This period marked a dramatic shift in the US labour market and economy, in that the established system began to crack. With the recession, temporary staffing agencies were called upon to carry much of the burden of layoffs, outsourcing and externalization of the workforce. The gold watch and the loyal handshake became cultural items of the past, while 'self-reliance' and 'entrepreneurship' became in vogue.

The US never had a public employment service with a monopoly, and temporary job placement was therefore seen as one among many forms of temporary or 'contingent' work. Different forms of contingent work have long been widespread in the US labour market. However, there is reason to believe that the temporary staffing industry in the US, which was already in place by the 1920s, has played an important structuring role in flexibilizing the labour supply under tight job-market conditions. Peck and Theodore argue that temporary staffing agencies have assumed an important and ongoing macro-regulatory role in the US labour market. Temporary staffing agencies, they argue, provide a means 'to manage and dissipate the effects of product market/personnel fluctuations, to tap skills required on a discontinuous basis, and to establish a form of at-will employment relationship among some segments of the labour supply' (Peck and Theodore 2007: 172). Temporary staffing agencies should not be understood primarily as largely passive actors facilitating a simple matching of labour supply and demand, but should instead be viewed as active intermediaries in the job market. The role of the temporary staffing industry in shaping the US labour should be understood as evolving to a great extent from a succession of court rulings and the related activities of industry lobbying, which have been crucial in the establishment of a regulatory settlement favourable to the growth of agency-mediated temping (Peck and Theodore 2002: 146–147).

There are today no binding regulations concerning the temporary help industry at the federal level, and only few minor regulations at state and local level. The impact of collective agreements is scant; only a fraction of workers in the temporary employment business are unionized and unions have had little success in attempting to influence the regulation of temporary agency work (Sweeney 2006). However, the temporary agency has since 1971 been legally the employer of the temporary employee, assuming responsibility for tax collection, making insurance contributions and handling compensation claims.

Yet another striking feature for the US temporary employment market is that, while a large portion of the workforce, an estimated one-third, is on short-term contracts, relatively few of these work through temporary agencies, about two per cent of the nation as a whole (CIETT 2005). As Peck and Theodore ask, 'Why should the heavily "deregulated" US labor market be less "temped out" than that of any other advanced industrial nation?' This is indeed an interesting question. Their answer rests on the idea that the potential demand for temps in the US may be dampened because the 'mainstream' employment relation is already relatively deregulated and because the labour market is already substantially flexibilized (see also Robinson 1999, Kalleberg 2000). The 'independent contractor', 'the free agent' and the 'consultant' have long been central figures in the US economy and labour market, not least in the booming Silicon Valley area. In Sweden, where the labour market is relatively less flexibilized, temporary agencies fulfil a more clearly defined role as legitimate intermediaries who facilitate and smooth the flexibilization of the labour market.

Around fifty-three per cent of the US temporary agency workforce are women and close to fifty per cent are under the age of 35 (Bureau of Labor Statistics, February 2005). The temporary agency workforce contains a higher than average proportion of immigrants than the workforce as a whole, as well as a higher proportion of people with no education beyond the high-school diploma.[11]

The number of temporary agency companies exploded in the Silicon Valley area in the mid-1980s, partly due to the economic downturn that the area experienced. The number of people employed in temporary staffing agencies nearly tripled between 1994 and 1998, and by the turn of the millennium came to represent 3.5 per cent of total employment in Silicon Valley (Benner 2002: 102–103). As Benner rightly points out, this number significantly understates the number of people that actually use temporary agencies at different times, since many move from temporary into permanent positions. He estimates that between seven and ten per cent of the workforce in Silicon Valley are likely to be employed by a temporary help agency at some point during the course of a single year, and that up to 40 per cent of the region's workforce is involved in non-standard employment relationships (Benner 2002: 38, 103). Rapid turnover has become the norm and even people in 'permanent employment' have to live with changing skill requirements, constant organizational change and ongoing needs for learning. While clerical and administrative support positions still form over a half of all temporary agency placements, this percentage is declining, with a concomitant expansion into technical, professional and managerial fields. This trend reflects as well the overall character of the business in Silicon Valley, with a high concentration of knowledge and technology intensive industries. I recognized this trend myself during my fieldwork in the Silicon Valley area, not only in the job positions my informants occupied, but also in the general attitude to temping, as closer to 'self-employment' and to 'consultancy work', than to the notion of 'the marginalized temp'.

So, in brief, the US temping business has evolved from being largely unregulated to carving out a distinct and growing niche for itself through successive lobbying, court cases and state-level regulations. Temps earn their salaries on an hourly basis and have to earn their rights to job security and social benefits through long-term employment with the temp agency.

Layered regulation

The differences, outlined above, between the three national contexts recall the importance of placing regulatory changes within a wider perspective, and giving consideration in particular to the effects of distinctive types of temporary agency employment regulation and State policies on the cultural construction of the flexible temporary agency worker. The differing institutional contexts, with Sweden's coordinated market economy on the one hand, and the liberal market economies (albeit with significant differences) of the UK and the US on the other, represent different cases in relation to the ways in which temporary flexible work is addressed and regulated. While all countries position the permanent contract as the norm, there are major differences as to what extent this policy has been pursued by the State, and how and by whom non-permanent, temporary work is regulated. In Sweden, there has long been a strong labour market regulation in place, resting on ILO conventions, statutory law and collective bargaining, and the move has been towards a deregulation of the market for temporary industries. In the UK, the already unregulated area of temporary employment promotes a more 'defensive' flexibility than the Swedish – one that is more strongly associated with a neoliberal labour market strategy and with declining scope for State control and trade union interference. The American case is one in which soft and partial regulation, and minimal State intervention and collective agreements leave the temporary employment business largely open to the promotion of flexible organizational solutions.

These influences on the construction of the flexible temporary agency worker interweave in complex ways. The tripartite relation between the temporary employment agency, the worker, and the user or client thus articulates differently across national contexts, with various expectations and perspectives attached to its parties. The similarities stem from the wide diffusion of a flexibility discourse with strong market-oriented undertones of individual entrepreneurship and freedom, intensively fuelled by temporary agencies.

With increasing globalization, other organizations as well have come to play a role in the regulation of the temping industry. During 2000 and early 2001 the European social partners were negotiating a framework agreement on standards for temporary agency work which failed in May 2001 (see Harvey 2002). After consulting the relevant European-level associations representing this sector, the Commission proposed a directive in March 2002 (CEC 2002). The proposed directive aimed to improve the working conditions of temporary employees, whilst providing a step in the harmonization of the European labour market. The directive makes it clear that temporary employees shall receive at least as favourable treatment, in terms of basic working and employment conditions, as a comparable worker in the user enterprise, unless the difference in treatment is justified by objective reasons (CEC 2002: 21). At the same time, the directive aims to establish a suitable framework for the use of temporary work to contribute to the smooth functioning of the labour and employment market (CEC 2002: 19).[12]

Whilst ILO played a role in the post-Second World War regulatory development, it has now taken on a 'softer' approach. A new, and more liberal, convention drafted in 1997 aimed to provide standards for private job placement. Its success, in terms of ratification, has hitherto been limited. ILO also passed a recommendation, mainly involving ethical codes of conduct for the temporary staffing business as well as a plea for more cooperation between public and private employment offices (Friberg et al. 2000: 25–26). The OECD has also on several occasions engaged in the regulation of temporary staffing, pushing for a liberalization of existing practices and regulations (OECD 1995, 1997).

From within the industry itself, branch associations have played crucial roles in lobbying for voluntary forms of regulation and in setting up codes of conduct. In the UK, the temporary staffing services are members of FRES (The Federation of Recruitment and Employment Services). FRES provides a yearly outline of the business and has created ethical codes of conduct for staffing services. In Sweden, temporary staffing services were, at the time of my fieldwork, organized by SPUR (Swedish Association of Temporary Work Businesses and Staffing Services). In 2003, the Swedish Association of Staff Agencies (Bemanningsföretagen), the employers and industry association for staffing and recruiting agencies in Sweden, replaced SPUR. The Swedish Association of Staff Agencies is part of Almega (an association for the support of service companies in Sweden) and the Confederation of Swedish Enterprise (Svenskt Näringsliv). The Swedish Association of Staff Agencies stands behind the issuing of ethical codes of conduct for the business as a whole (www.almega.se, visited 15 July 2007). The UK and the Swedish branch organizations are, in turn, members of the European organization CIETT (International Confederation of Temporary Work Businesses). CIETT organizes 21 national branch organizations and works to promote the interests of the business in the EU (www.ciett.org, visited 15 July 2007). The American Staffing Association (ASA) – previously National Association of Temporary and Staffing Services (NATS) – promotes legal, ethical, and professional practices for the staffing industry in the US. ASA and its affiliated chapters promote the interests of the industry through legal and legislative advocacy, public relations, education and the establishment of codes of ethical conduct (www.americanstaffing. net, visited 15 July 2007).[13]

Hence, the temporary staffing business is one criss-crossed by various regulatory forms, binding as well as voluntary, national as well as transnational. It would be too simplistic here to talk about a deregulation of the business in general, since only partially and only in Sweden has a proper deregulation taken place. It would also be much too simple to speak about the area as one of predominantly 'private authority structures' of 'soft law' forms of regulation, since there are as well binding state and federal legislations in place, to varying degrees and in varying forms (cf. Djelic and Sahlin Andersson 2004). I would suggest instead that we are dealing with a layered form of regulation, or rather governance, in which voluntary forms of regulation, such as codes of conduct and recommendations, are laid on top of, or compensate for, binding national state regulations or international conventions.[14]

Hence, despite the global spread of temporary staffing agencies, the local working conditions and employment contracts may vary a great deal across countries. Olsten, the corporation in focus in this book, has itself to be flexible enough to adapt to the regional variations in business specialization and in regulation.

2
Into the Temping Zone

First steps

Megan is on her way to the Office Angels temping agency in Leeds. It is a chilly spring morning, and the streets are buzzing with the energy of the early morning traffic. She hurries her steps towards the Headrow office. She wouldn't want to be late for her first meeting with the temporary staffing agency. Having left secondary school last year and then tried odd jobs here and there without much luck, she has set her hopes on temping. Perhaps temping can help support her in-between now and making a career choice? Perhaps an interesting and tempting job offer may even turn up? Admittedly, she was not very keen on turning to temping a few weeks ago. There are, in her mind, a number of uncertainties attached to temping. Who knows where one may end up, or what kinds of assignments one may be sent on? Would she stand the test? And then there is the ambivalence attached to the status of 'the temp', as the free agent answering to no one, on the one hand, and as the one on the lowest step on the corporate ladder, on the other.

Well, here she is, standing before the Office Angels entrance door, her expectations highly set and keen on getting a first assignment. As she enters, she walks straight towards the reception desk, where she is greeted by the receptionist. Megan has an appointment with one of the assignment coordinators, and the receptionist asks her to take a seat while waiting. Normally, the assignment coordinator will not receive everyone interested in applying for a job, since competition in the area is tough. As a new applicant, though, Megan is hardly aware of this fact. She is a little bit nervous.

In the waiting area next to the entrance, there is coffee and soft drinks, as well as an assortment of magazines for distraction. Megan pours herself a cup of coffee and picks up a magazine randomly. Shortly, she is asked to fill in a registration form while waiting, with all the details possible about the type of job applied for, skills in typing, previous job experience, preferences in type of firm, and other details. The receptionist emphasizes that references are very important and are always checked and one should be able to give at least two.

The receptionist then asks Megan to go through a couple of tests, involving spelling, visual accuracy, typing and the like. The receptionist then makes a classification of her skills according to the test results. Without much ado, she takes a quick picture of Megan, which is then attached to the registration form, the test results and her CV. Having her picture taken, the receptionist tells her with a smile, may make her feel a bit uncomfortable, but the picture is valuable to have when possible candidates for a particular assignment are discussed. It may provide the client what that extra bit of information and the personal touch needed to get the job.

When the candidate has gone through this procedure, it is time for the interview with one of the assignment coordinators. The interview lasts about 10 to 15 minutes, and Megan is then given a folder, a personal wallet called 'Welcome to Office Angels', with information on administrative routines, such as how to fill in timesheets, pay day and cheque cashing, insurance and so on. In this wallet is also enclosed the folder 'An Introduction to Temping with Office Angels'.

It happens that the candidate is offered an assignment during the interview itself, but the normal procedure is for the assignment coordinator to check references carefully before giving an offer. Usually, this is a fairly quick procedure, and there are ready-made forms to fill in to facilitate the process. If the candidate proves to be promising and there is a job opening available, an offer is normally given within a few days. On the other hand, there are large numbers of applicant registration forms never matched with an assignment archived in the office.

Megan passes the interview without any real difficulties. She has been rehearsing possible questions for herself, and has been given some advice by a friend who has been through this procedure before. The interviewer has also gained quite a favourable impression of Megan during the short interview. The candidate seemed to be prepared for what the job takes – a lot of self-discipline, flexibility, readiness to learn and to adapt to work environments. She also seemed to have a good sense of humour, which may come in handy at times, and a sociable personality. The test also proves that her language use is rather good, that she has sufficient typing skills, although not outstanding, and that she knows the basics of word processing.

Megan's first encounter with the agency ends with the assignment coordinator asking Megan to step into her cubicle for a while, informing her about the results of the test and that they are interested in having her work for them as a temp, particularly on administrative assignments involving reception work, project administration, and the like. The assignment coordinator lets Megan know they may be calling her shortly, within a couple of days, when they have found the right match for her.

Megan leaves the agency premises with a smile on her face. The whole thing went rather well, she thinks. If the right assignment turns up, she is willing to give it a try.

Across the world, women and men are continuously applying for jobs through temporary employment agencies. In Leeds, in Santa Clara, in California, and in Stockholm, where I spent some time doing fieldwork at Olsten Corporation, as well as in Palermo, Tokyo, Brisbane or Nairobi, people set their hopes on temp agencies. And they come with a variety of motives.

In this chapter we will take a look at some of the motives that draw people into flexible temporary work, the kinds of reasons they have for temping, and the imagined trajectories they carry with them. Their motives and imaginings are then balanced by the demands of the temp agency and the client organizations, as they continue their work trajectories. I will also discuss how I myself entered the field of temping as a researcher, what challenges the field posited for me, and how I engaged with these.

Why temping?

Temporary employment agencies use a lot of energy and rhetoric in trying to attract candidates to work for them. Their marketing campaigns often cater to dreams, to the future, and to bright careers. In attracting possible candidates, temp agencies work with promising scenarios. Temping is 'a hot ticket to career success', 'a stepping stone to the career of your dreams', opening the doors 'to a world of exciting job opportunities' (see, for example, Rogers 1996). Temping, according to agency representatives, can empower individuals to get a head start in their careers and to take control of their own career development, and open up possibilities for new, more flexible ways of working. According to the folder 'A job to love', a job as a 'consultant' at Olsten in Sweden offers you excitement, personal development, challenges and individual reward.

In marketing campaigns, flexibility is portrayed as being in the hands of the candidate. In the flexible job market, you can 'work when you want, be free when you want', 'work when you want, be with your kids when you want'.[1] Flexibility is here repositioned as involving an array of opportunities and a space for freedom in which one may navigate according to one's personal priorities. Recruitment ads portray the flexible job market as opening up avenues for exploration, empowerment and freedom. Flexibility comes across as an 'enchanted' environment (cf. Schneider 1993). In this sense, flexibility is yet another version of the many utopias constructed around work and the empowered worker (Grey and Garsten 2002). Flexibility, by way of its capacity to carry a diverse set of meanings, works both as a liberator and as a powerful regime of control.

An assignment coordinator in Santa Clara also conveyed something of the enchantment of flex work:

> Working as a temp may be tough at times, since you never really now what your day is going to look like. Some people find this hard and stressful. On the other hand, if you are up to it, you can actually tailor your own worklife pretty much. It all boils down to what you want. I could give you lots of examples where people have climbed the ladder and eventually got a permanent position somewhere at a client's. Through temping, you expose yourself to a lot of opportunities, you really do. It's up to you what you do with these.

People are drawn into flexible, temporary work for all sorts of reasons. At base, temping is a way to earn a livelihood, to get a job, even if temporary, and to support oneself and one's family. 'Choice' may not always be the correct term to use when speaking of reasons for temping. People in the temping industry have not all 'chosen' to be there. As with all sorts of work, temporary work provides an income, as well as connecting people to a community of workmates, and can, in the best of cases, provide a sense of meaning beyond the mere performance of tasks. Temporary jobs are, to a growing extent, what is offered to a lot of jobseekers. Indeed, moving into the temping zone may not so much be about picking and choosing from a great variety of jobs on a smorgasbord, as a way of earning a living. This is, however, often concealed behind the managerial understanding and marketing of temporary work as being of a voluntary nature (cf. Collinson 1987: 380). The notion of choice tends to serve as an ideological control mechanism for obscuring the realities of circumscribed mobility, auditability and self-reliance.

Beyond basic material reasons for temping, there may be other, complementary rationalities at work. These are not cut loose from the enchanted, managerial rhetoric of flexibility, but interlinked to and referring to them. Here, we may utilize Appadurai's (1996) conception of 'imagination as a social practice', which he argues to be a critical aspect of globalization processes. The dreams, visions and imaginings that people construct in their everyday lives may not, and are not, always in line with the structural, material conditions that define temporary, flexible work in globalizing labour markets. Rather, we may expect there to be varying degrees of disjuncture and friction, and the imaginings and the structures to articulate in curious ways with each other.

During my research into this area, I met with women and men who came to work with temporary agencies for a variety of different reasons. Indeed, there seem to be as many reasons for temping as there are people who temp. It is, however, possible to discern a number of motives that appear more frequently than others. And these have to do with the imaginings of getting a real job, advancing one's career, changing the balance of work to life, in short – of promising future scenarios, and aspirations realized. Let's have a look at some of the things that motivate people to join the temporary workforce!

Opting for the alternative

For a relatively long time now, we have been living with the permanent, regular, full-time employment contract as an ideal. This ideal has served to draw the lines between the unemployed and the employed, to set up incentives for action, and to organize measures for the reintroduction of those outside the labour market. Many of us have been geared to the goal of getting a steady job, even when that might have put a spoke in the wheel for a more experimental and dynamic worklife.

The very image of work and employment as long-term, durable and predictable provides something of a backdrop against which temporary employees construct their relation to temporary, flexible work. They tend to judge the merits and drawbacks of temporary work against the ideal of permanent work contracts. For some, this ideal is seen as connoting a career-oriented life, with a certain stability and orderliness to it. It brings to mind steady family life and a traditional breadwinner ideology. And it creates a degree of stress of not living up to expectations, of not being able to get the position one aspires to, of being trapped, perhaps prematurely, in a middle-class way of life. This kind of perspective was often seen among the younger temps, those who had recently graduated from college or university, who were single and basically career-oriented. Many of them talked of 'not being ready for a career yet', wanting to 'see what's out there before I decide'. For them, temping is an alternative to the conventional lifelong employment contract.

Temps usually see their job as something distinctively different from a regular one. It lacks the long-term commitment and loyalty that is usually associated with regular employment. In many ways, temping thus seen is a 'job-not' (Rogers 1996: 40). Rather, it is an alternative to the regular job, and a space for learning and experimenting with what a career might entail. It also allows for a more relaxed relation with the employing agency, in that there is little in the way of long-term commitment. Temping is also perceived as attractive, since it offers flexibility in the sense of variation and change, the opportunity to get acquainted with different kinds of workplaces, types of business and companies and different tasks. It offers a chance to change workplace, jobs or business.

Dreaming of freedom

The flexibility associated with temping also carries the potential for freedom. When asked about the advantages of temping, temps themselves often refer to the freedom of movement that it offers them. Niklas, one of Olsten's temps in Sweden, thinks that temping is a flexible job arrangement, because 'it's easier to take a break' and the job allows him to take leave to travel around the world. Being in his late twenties, Niklas is keen to travel and to have a job that allows him to do just that. He thinks that a regular, permanent job just does not offer the same sense of freedom.

In fact, the prospect of defining one's own career, of deciding on one's patterns of movement and working hours – of enjoying the freedom associated with flexible work – was one of the recurring themes of my informants. Often, the flexibility that comes with temping was described as involving a greater degree of freedom than a regular job would do. By the end of each assignment, there was an array of opportunities; of getting a better assignment, of not taking another assignment at all, or taking a break from work to engage in other, more interesting activities.

However, this potentiality is seldom realized. Niklas and many others with him nurture the idea of freedom while going about their everyday work at the client's. Once you are into temping, it is not always that easy to ask for leave, or to say 'no' to an assignment because the hours do not fit exactly with your own plan. Niklas had been with Olsten for about six months when I met him, and had not yet made use of the freedom he was looking for, nor did he have any more precise plans for when he might do so. But the idea was still alive.

Others have chosen to do temping because it allows them to spend more time nurturing their interests. Susanne, working for Olsten in Santa Clara, has her mind set on becoming an actor and takes evening classes in drama. Temping to her is ideal, 'since it doesn't take up too much of my creative energy', as she puts it, allowing her a relative degree of freedom to engage in what is more important for her. She is not too keen to climb the ladder and to take on more demanding temp jobs, since that would ultimately distract from her focus on acting and drain her of energy. She prefers to do receptionist work or low-skilled clerical work. This leaves room for other, more engaging activities, she tells me.

Eva is a single, 27 year old woman who works with Olsten as a receptionist. She is well educated, with a marketing diploma from the UK and several years of working abroad, in the UK and in Malaysia. Still, she has found it hard to get a regular job in marketing. Swedish employers seem not to value her international experience, she tells me somewhat disappointedly. After some time of intense jobhunting, she turned to Olsten in Stockholm. Now that she has been working with them for eight months, she values their capacity to place her with clients, but is not prepared to commit herself to them for long:

> I am a little bit restless. I don't want to feel that I have got stuck somewhere, because then it would feel like: Now it's all over and I have to grow up. Both my parents worked for the same employer all their lives. Got a gold watch for 30 years of loyal public service. That frightens me a bit. That's not how things work any longer. It's all projects. That's how it works.[2]

In the above, Eva describes temping as an alternative kind of employment, as one involving more freedom from loyalty and commitment, but she also points to what she perceives as a change in the way work in general is organized, towards more project-based work and greater degrees of contingency.

Flexible schedules

Some people take advantage of the flexibility offered through temping by only accepting the assignments that suit them. These are usually people who are not dependent on the income as such, but who prefer to work 'for social reasons', 'to do something more meaningful than staying at home', 'to bring some extra money into the household', or for similar kinds of reasons. Laureen, who works for Olsten in Santa Clara, tells me she does not really need to work, since her husband earns enough money to support them both. She has spent years at home, tending to their children and their house, but now that the kids are old enough to take care of themselves, she finds being a housewife just 'too boring'. She enjoys meeting new people, getting to know new work environments, and since she and her husband no longer have financial dependants, she can always turn down an offer that does not meet her expectations. This gives her a certain feeling of integrity and power in relation to the agency, of which she is aware. 'Most young girls are not in my position to negotiate assignments', she says, 'but have to adapt to what they can get. So in this sense, I think I am in a fortunate position.'

There is another, less powerful position associated with flexible schedules as well. Temporary, flexible work is often presented, by temp agency representatives and by many women themselves, as ideally suited to women's multiple roles as caretakers, homemakers and wage earners. In this way, the temping agency fosters a 'motherly work culture', in which caring, tending to the family, and contributing to the male breadwinner ideology play a significant part (Hochshild 1997: 20). In this way, the 'feminization' in process in flexible work involves a strengthening of male–female cultural stereotypes as well as a structural move towards the insertion of women into temporary, flexible jobs.

Temping may thus be viewed as providing an alternative for women whose domestic roles make regular, full-time work and career impossible. Often, it is seen as a way out of domestic duties when children have grown more independent and boredom lurks in the empty home. It is, in other words, offered as a way to tailor women's work to the dominant role of the male breadwinner (cf. Freeman 2000: 46). Only here, the role of the female employee becomes one associated with contingent work contracts, lower positions, lower rates of pay and minimal benefits, at least in the UK and the US, where temporary workers do not enjoy the same contractual and social benefits as their counterparts in Sweden. Dora, who works for Office Angels in Leeds, tells me how she tries to strike a balance between her household duties and the need to earn extra income for the household, which is not always an easy balancing act. Her experience is one of being torn between different demands. Flexible work for her is not so much about tailoring a flexible schedule that suits her, but trying to balance her husband's desires with those of the agency.

Often, temping is associated with the possibility of defining one's own working hours. As evinced in the advertisement above, 'Work when you want, be free when you want', the idea is that flexible work entails a certain control over one's working time. A large proportion of the informants claim either to enjoy the frequent change of tasks

and environment, of being able to take spells off between assignments, or to have commitments which make continuous working
impossible. Mildred, at the Leeds agency, says she chose to apply for
work with Office Angels to a large extent because she wanted the
opportunity to tailor working hours to her own demands. She has a
small child, and does not want to feel that she is entirely in the hands
of her employer as regards working time. However, even though
there is, at least theoretically, the possibility to negotiate about an
assignment, as well as to reject an offer, she admits to shying away
from doing so because she realizes it might not be easy for the client
to adjust to her wishes. Moreover, she does not want to jeopardize
her future with Office Angels.

Temping also allows for part-time solutions for those who prefer
this. The temporary staffing agency can organize part-time solutions
and jobsharing more easily than an individual employee or any
employer could. By having access to a pool of people waiting for an
assignment, the agency can promise to fill vacancies and solve a
part-time request without too much trouble.

The temp agency as springboard

The temping industry harbours a large number of young people, who
have just completed upper secondary school or got their university
degree, and who hope that the temp agency will be able to assist
them in getting their first experiences of work in an interesting
organization. Rather than looking for a job through the public
employment service, or responding to a job advertisement in the
press, they rely on the temp agency to place them on assignments. In
this sense, the temp agency plays the role of a springboard for people
who are just about to start their careers.

Kate, who works from the Santa Clara office, has a Bachelors degree
in marine fisheries, on top of which she has taken secretarial classes
and evening classes in computing, tells me why she entered the
flexible job market:

> *Kate*: This was a long-term plan and I really prepared myself and
> even to this day I'm still in school. I'm taking classes in a com-
> munity college. It's just to upgrade my skills but no particular
> degree. Just updating skills wherever I can.
> *Christina*: What position would you like to have in five years time?

Kate: I'd say... Well actually at this stage I'm going though a career assessment. I have a career assessment class every Thursday, because at this point I thought I'd really better try and find out what exactly it is I'd like to eventually spend time on from, you know, five, ten, years from now. And I haven't decided, you know, because... I like computers and I'd like to have my own business and, you know, a lot of factors... and of course you know I'd like to start a family and all that. But I would say... being like a manager, sort of like a manager. Ehm, not exactly a manager, I'd say. Like an assistant to a manager or something, but not high (*laughter*)... I'd say I want a career.

The idea of using the temping agency as a springboard was prominent among the more well-educated temps and among the more explicitly career-oriented ones. For some, the temping agency was seen as a resource in that it might assist them in climbing further up the career ladder. Dora, a 35 year old woman who works for Olsten in Santa Clara, calls herself a Human Resource consultant and aims to start her own consultancy. She intends to make use of the temping agency to place her with interesting clients, so that she can learn the job and get experienced before starting her own business.

For people like Dora and Angel, the temping agency is in command of resources that they themselves are not. The agency has the organizational capacity, the experience, the networks and the mandate to push careers further. The agency in this way acts as a lever for them and projects a timeline and a trajectory for their future careers.

The temp agency as mediator

Temp agencies act rather like switchboards in the organizational landscape, with their vast network links to client organizations and job opportunities. Agency coordinators are in a strong position to mediate between those in need of a job and those in need of manpower, something that is well recognized among the temps. Some of them join the temporary workforce with a view to taking advantage of this network to get ahead in their careers, find more challenging jobs, change the work environment, or change business sector.

Cathy is an experienced middle-aged woman who works through Olsten in Santa Clara. Before getting in touch with Olsten, she spent

20 years in retail management. Two years ago she left her job to take six months off and 'see what was out there in the field'. She is now in the computing business as an executive assistant. This is what she tells me about the beginning of her employment with Olsten:

> *Cathy*: I had just quit a job I didn't really like, and wasn't sure what to do next. And so I went to Olsten. Went on one or another assignment and landed here and haven't left for almost two years, a year and a half (*laughter*). So. And I've used Olsten before. In between little spots that you're not working or during college. But all of it has been in retail management or fast-food management. It's a Monday to Friday job for me.
>
> *Christina*: What kind of positions have you had?
>
> *Cathy*: My last one was assistant store manager at Target, which is a discount chain here and that was the number one store of that company up in the San Francisco area. Ah … but in retail in the US you kind of, kind of alternate between different retailers and you get promoted here and there, but basically I started out during college, cashier type of thing, and then went into management programme out of college twenty years ago or whatever (*laughter*). Went into management. Hit 40 and well, decided life's too short for this (*laughter*) so let's do something different!
>
> *Christina*: You just wanted a change?
>
> *Cathy*: Right, right. And I used Olsten, thinking 'OK, I'll go to all these big companies', you know. The ideal is, work for Apple, work for these big companies that are supposed to have all these great things for the employees and stuff. Ended up here in a small company. Liked the people. Training on a computer was a big thing because I knew the retail networking but not what Windows was or anything at all, so I mean I've come a long way with that and it's been a big help. Just a complete change from what I was doing.
>
> *Christina*: Did you know you wanted to go into the computing industry?
>
> *Cathy*: No, no. I just kind of wanted basically to get to a Monday to Friday type of job. In retail where I was working you work seven days a week, you're on call 24 hours a day. And I wanted to change. Basically wanted to get into personnel, but knew

that you needed to have at least some computer skills, so when I first came here I also was going to junior college and taking some self-paid computer classes a little, but so I could at least talk the lingo.

Temping can often serve to mediate between different jobs and different organizations, and facilitate the change in life that is wished for. Many of my informants spoke in terms of 'using the temp agency' to make change happen. The agency stands at a convenient point of location for the individual, with the vast network of client contacts providing a valuable resource. To get into that network, to get at the resources, the individual chooses to approach the agency.

In the Silicon Valley, I was often told how the attractive high-tech companies could be approached through the mediation of the agency alone. 'They will never hire you directly unless you're a star management person', Mike told me, 'but you can try to get in through a temp agency.' Mike had himself been wanting to get into one of the computer game producers in the area, and approached them directly, only to be told that yes, they might consider employing him for a period of time, but only on a temporary basis and through Olsten, since they would not take any 'headcount' risks.

In the organizational landscape, temps are favourably positioned with regard to client organizations and job vacancies. For the individual looking for a job, temp agencies can establish the contact, provide the client with a favourable and packaged image of the employee, and mediate in negotiations. The role of temp agencies as mediators between client organizations and individuals should not be underestimated. Client organizations, on their part, trust the agencies to do their job well, to find them a suitable candidate, in time, and with no strings attached. They avoid the risks of taking on 'headcount' that may turn out both a 'misfit' and too costly.

Getting a 'real job'

Casey (1987: 82) reports that, according to the numerous surveys conducted by temp agencies US, a substantial proportion of temps are looking for permanent jobs, but some of these are also using their experience of temporary jobs to sort out what kind of job they would like. The same has been said about the US and Sweden. However statistics are somewhat contradictory and shifting on this point.

There are also many debates over the extent to which the temporary agency workforce is composed of people actively choosing this form of work. Agencies are quick to identify themselves in terms of their 'intermediary function', fulfilling the needs of particular groups of workers, such as women returning to the labour market, youngsters, and people with other commitments. According to most statistical data, however, the majority of temp workers *would* prefer a permanent job.

In my research, a large majority of the temps I interviewed and talked to – about eighty per cent – said they wanted to have a regular full-time job in about five years' time. However, when we talked this over in a more detailed and nuanced way, it emerged that having an employment contract *per se* was often less important than having a stable workplace to go to, where they could develop stronger social ties with colleagues. It was thus the mobility and the location of work that mattered most, in that they were seen to relate to social work relations and a sense of community at work. Moreover, in Sweden most of my informants already had regular permanent employment contracts with the agency. Even so, they reported wanting a 'real job' later on, explaining that a real job was one in which they did not have to ambulate between locations.

Many of the temps told me they wanted to get a regular job because that would include them in the community of workers at a particular site. Janice, in Leeds, started to work in the temping industry right after her graduation from college. She said she had the idea that work would also bring one friends and colleagues and a sense of belonging somewhere. Through work, one would be able to feel that one's own contribution was part of a collective effort. 'But when temping, I don't really get to see that, since I'm out of here before the results are visible. And that's why my workmates at the client's don't really feel like colleagues. If I had a real job I don't think I would feel that way.'

The established notion of the 'real job' which is regular and permanent is still there as the norm and backdrop against which all other kinds of job contracts are valued. The changes in perceptions of job and work may have shifted somewhat over the last decades towards a more multifaceted perception of what a job, or work, can be like (see, for example, Rifkin 1995, and Pink 2001 , for 'strong' market-oriented versions of these transformations). Allvin (2004) argues that, more than anything, work has become more individual-ized, 'juridicalized' and contract guided. With changes in produc-tion systems and work organization, rules regulating participation in work change. And, as the rules change, so does the conception of the individual in relation to work, towards a self-reliant operator in a market. In the temping business, this would be true for many employ-ees. However, tied up with the notion of a 'real job' are expectations of a sense of stability and community, as well as of a clearer career trajectory.

Angela had been working with Olsten in Santa Clara for five months when I met her. She had given up a regular job and career in the health sector, where she had worked for nine years. Her hopes were set on finding another regular job contract through Olsten.

> *Angela*: I used to work for just one company as a permanent employee since I moved to the US from the Philippines and I thought that there's a lot of change going on here in technol-ogy. That I should keep brisk or stay on top of things about what's going on here in the market. So, I thought this would be a good way to go out there and see, you know, what the compa-nies are up to and still be able to earn a living. ... I have a degree in biology, so I should be able to find something in the technology business.
>
> I really take in and study the whole environment and I take note of the company I am interested in. If I'm interested I would apply for a job. But so far, at this point, I'd like to give myself more of a chance to experience a lot of companies. ... The com-panies keep extending me, so I know they are interested in me. I had a couple of companies that I worked for, and every time their employees go on vacation they would call and ask spe-cifically for me. And sometimes they would come up and say: 'Why don't you leave us your résumé or an application?' For me, it's flattering to know that people are interested in me, and so I started assessing my skills, and I'd say: 'Well, I'm not bad at all', you know, to be able to get people interested like that!
>
> *Christina*: Could you do that? Could you leave your résumé and apply for a job while working for Olsten?
>
> *Angela*: Yes, actually, Olsten is very open to that. A lot of people use temporary agencies as a transition until they find a

permanent job and often their staff is understanding. A couple of months ago I had the same situation. Someone had offered me a job and then it didn't work out, but I was already temping for them, and so I had to come back. And they said: 'Oh, we understand. That's what people use us for when they're going through transition.'

Career temping

Temping can also be made into a career in itself. Especially if you have a set of skills that are in demand in the labour market and if you become known as a reliable, competent person with a unique competence. Whereas I seldom heard this being expressed in Stockholm, and quite rarely in Leeds, it was not uncommon for Santa Clara temps to air this view. Hilary, for example, is a woman in her mid-thirties, who has her mind geared to becoming a consultant in demand. When asked if she wanted to set up her own consultancy, she says, 'No, it is far better for me to use the services of Olsten. I count on remaining a temp for quite some. This is my job now.'

Most of the temps I interviewed and who wanted to do 'career temping' said they did not start their work with Olsten thinking of doing it as a career. However, on the way, they discovered some attractive features in temping that made them change their mind. Often, it was after being put on the 'A-list' of high-performing, reliable temps, and having been offered a permanent position with the client a few times, that they realized this was the kind of lifestyle they actually wanted. Career temping was talked about as an option for those who want some flexibility in their working lives, who want to keep the door open to other opportunities – and still be successful and climb the ladder of pay and position. Hilary also told me she did not want to wake up one day with a 'pink tie' around her neck. Career temping provides her with opportunities to meet new people, learn new skills, broaden her client base and frees her from 'office politics'.

Even if it was in the Silicon Valley that I came across most of the career-oriented temps, this was also where the drawbacks of career temping were most harshly felt: the lack of healthcare benefits, life insurance programmes and pension plans. For the same reasons career temps have a stronger interest in staying on with the same temp agency. By doing so, they can earn their right to fuller benefits through long-term employment, since the regulatory system in the

US does not automatically grant temporary employees the same right to benefits as regular employees.[3]

Imaginary trajectories

In the work of temping, imagination as a social practice plays a crucial role. It is a form of negotiation between the individual as a site of agency and the locally and globally defined fields of possibility that flexible work opens up, and close. Imagination is central to the form of agency that is cultivated in the temporary business and a key component in fashioning the flexible employee. The translocal processes of 'making up' the flexible employee involve the carving out of motives, negotiating differences between temps' motives and the agency's motives, and creating a certain sense of 'agency' in relation to the fluctuations of labour market demand. Through the work of imagination, global pressures are reduced to small, comprehensible parts which may be dealt with by invoking 'motive' and 'agency'. Imaginations serve to guide temps along their trajectories and to provide a sense of coherence with notions of career and community. In Appadurai's words, 'the work of the imagination ... is neither purely emancipatory nor entirely disciplined but is a space of contestation in which individuals and groups seek to annex the global into their own practices of the modern' (1996: 4).

In the foregoing paragraphs, a number of different reasons for temping have been given. There are yet others. People join the temporary staffing business for a multitude of reasons. A general observation is that my informants seldom talked about 'mere chance', 'force' or 'luck' when recounting their ways into the business. In part, this may be due to the interview situation itself, which may have prompted a more 'rational' reply than would otherwise have been the case. Even so, I believe that their actions are to a large part 'decision-interpreted' rather than 'decision-guided', in the sense that a search is made into what the decision might be, rather than weighing alternatives beforehand. This is what Weick calls 'retrospective sense-making' (Weick 1979). In his view, 'Careers usually turn out to be a set of actions that are career-interpreted after the fact rather than career-planned before the fact' (Weick 1979: 195). We should look at the reasons for entering the temp industry, as well the conceptions of career made in temping, from the perspective of retrospective sensemaking and interpretation. The retrospective sensemaking links up with the imaginings and aspirations of the temps, to sketch out a space in which they navigate their movements.

Flex work is by its very nature also a balancing act. Temping, apart from involving new imaginings, new opportunities to broaden one's experiences and knowledge repertoire, also involves new interdependencies and the subjugation of the individual to new kinds of regulations and measures of standardization. This may be seen throughout the employment cycle: in the first interview, over the course of assignments and evaluation procedures, in the upscaling or downscaling of types of assignments, and in salary levels. In the processes of recruitment and evaluation, the individual candidate goes through a series of steps that are predetermined and standardized. The kinds of skills and traits of character that are considered relevant and important for being a 'good temp' are already set by the agency. Candidates are evaluated and classified according to common, pre-defined categories that bear a close resemblance across countries and agency sites. It is partly through these standardized processes that the individual is constructed and framed as 'a temp' (cf. Goffman 1974).

Thus, the making of a flexible temporary agency worker entails the construction of a categorical identity fraught by contradictory discourses of the self. By this, I mean that while individual freedom of choice and empowerment are stressed, the individual is at the same time circumscribed by the implicit or explicit demands for adjustment to the collectivity of temps. There are expectations as well as regulations regarding temporary agency workers that to a great extent limit the degree of freedom to construct one's career trajectory. Flexibility has its limits, and the process of getting a temporary job is relatively standardized. The individual temp is caught up in organizational webs of interdependence with global reach.

The significance of this categorical shaping appears in full clarity when mirrored against the expectations of freedom from regularization and collectivization that the temps give expression to. For example, one of the temps at Office Angels, when asked her opinion on the role of unions in the temping business, strongly asserted that one of the reasons why she took a negative view of them was that she did not like to be 'regimented'. She was against any form of collective pressure and formation in her working life. Even so, we may argue that the very conditions under which she works act in the direction of regimentation, as a diffuse and uni-directional surveillance and production of order.

Moving into the temping zone thus involves matching one's imaginings, aspirations and hopes with the expectations, demands and requirements of the agency and the client organization. At the heart of my argument is the idea that the imaginings as well as the identities of temps are constructed in subtle (and sometimes not so subtle) ways that align them with organizational goals. In this alignment, flexible adaptation is both to do with performance and with surveillance. Employees are, at the same time, both active shapers of their trajectories and governed subjects, confronted with the need to become 'enterprising selves' (du Gay 1991, Miller and Rose 1995). Finding one's way in the temping business is to a great extent a matter of making sense of flexibility and discontinuity: of constructing one's own trajectory.

An anthropologist looks for the temping field

So we know something about how the temporary employees get into the temping zone. But how did I get there? For me, as a researcher, moving into the temping field was somewhat of a challenge. Where was I to place myself in a field that is continuously shifting, and where people join and leave at short notice? It seemed a bit like trying to catch running water in one's hands. Doing fieldwork by definition means locating oneself somewhere in space and time. In this sense, fieldwork is always local. But studying translocal organizations risks leaving one with the feeling that the sense of continuity, context and the experience of 'finding one's feet' (Geertz 1973) that are so much strived for, are jeopardized.

As I started to study the flexible job market, I was often confronted with the feeling that the really interesting processes – the conversations, the socializing, the conflicts – were going on somewhere else. This feeling was also linked to the idea that these were to be found at some particular place, and that I only had to find this place to get at the relevant information. In searching for the field, I was hoping to find the place where people made plans for the future, decisions about projects and careers, where relations were crafted and networks formed, resources negotiated about, and where the impact of larger structures could be seen (cf. Strathern 1995: 179).

Already at an early stage of my research, when doing pilot interviews with temporary employees and their managers in the Stockholm area, I came to realize that temping fields are not always easily located, and that doing fieldwork relies on certain assumptions regarding the nature of 'fields' and their boundaries. The new global economy has to be seen as 'a complex, overlapping and disjunctive order' (Appadurai 1997: 32), in which ethnographic fields overlap with each other. During these very first interviews, the interlinkages between the local branch offices and the headquarters in the US were evident. There were repeated mentions of the American influence in terms of corporate culture and origins. Clearly, organizational routines and practices in hiring and evaluation had been set up with templates provided by the headquarters. So I travelled to the headquarters in Melville, Long Island, to meet with senior management. I was also able to conduct a handful of interviews with people employed by the agency. Soon after, I went to Silicon Valley, California, where the ratio of temporary to permanent employees is substantially higher than the average in the US. It seemed to me a good idea to get into the whirlpool of dynamic labour market change and experimentation. From previous research and fieldwork, I had acquired a good knowledge of the area (see Garsten 1994). After initial contacts with management at the regional office in Santa Clara, I was given the opportunity to sit in during a couple of days in one of the local Silicon Valley offices.

From there, I would have the opportunity to follow the process of an applicant's first contact with Olsten through to their first assignment with a client organization. I was very happy to gain access to the inside of a temp agency, so to speak, and expectant as regards the observations I was hoping to make.

Early one morning, I got into my rented car and joined the heavy traffic on El Camino Real, the main road and communicative vein through the Silicon Valley, heading towards the local office where I was going to spend a few days doing participant observation. Despite the traffic, I thoroughly enjoyed the feeling of being one of the many thousands of people on their way to work, to an office, a store, or a car repair shop – to a place of work. After over an hour of driving, I stepped into the Olsten office and was greeted by Rose, one of the assignment coordinators. Rose was a neatly dressed and polite woman in her early thirties, with several years of experience in the industry. She offered me coffee and showed me around the premises. The office was functionally furnished, with four or five open-space workplaces. On each of these was a computer. On the walls there were information leaflets, children's drawings, and photographs of the families of employees. On the desks, there were files with work material and forms of various kinds. Everything was colour coordinated, in the discrete bluish-grey colours of Olsten. The four women working there as office staff were about the same age, professionally dressed and with graceful manners.

In a little while, I was shown to a desk in an adjacent meeting room, where Rose told me I could 'sit and work'. She left me with the assurance that I could approach her at any time, if I had questions. At the time, there were no job candidates in the office, but Rose and her colleagues were waiting for a few of the temps to stop by to take tests in computer literacy and to be interviewed for possible new assignments. I sat down and waited.

To begin with, it was convenient to have some time to get a good sense of the premises and to take notes on what had happened so far. Rose and Marie, her colleague, were working silently at their computers.

After a while, I started to get restless and walked around the office, offered to run errands for Marie, who willingly replied to my questions and showed me test forms for temps who wanted to upgrade their skills, and hopefully their wages. I was in the unusual situation of having to search for questions and for details to fill time with some sort of content.

When a couple of hours had passed in this way, the feeling of significant things happening somewhere else began to grow on me. If I were ever to locate 'the field', where interesting conversations were held, where social interactions were frequent, and where relations were worked on, well, I would need to go elsewhere. That place was certainly not here.

The absence of temps was striking. Now and then, one of the staff talked to a temp on the telephone, but it was of course difficult to figure out what the conversation was all about. A couple of women appeared during the course of the day to work at one of the computers allocated to them, and the mailman appeared once to deliver the mail. These visits broke the monotony for a few minutes. Doing fieldwork in a temp agency proved to be a rather boring venture. I soon realized that fieldwork under these circumstances, in this place, was not going to deliver much of interest.

Or perhaps it did? On second thoughts, I realized the world of flexible work might be just like this. A few people mediating contacts between candidates and clients via the telephone and the computer. Temps who seldom have face-to-face contact with the person mediating the assignment or with other temps who, formally, are their colleagues. People who move around from workplace to workplace and seldom spend more than a few days or weeks in the same office. A field of mediation and brokerage. If this was so, I had come somewhat closer to the character of the field itself.

Ethnography in fields of mediation

Methodologically, I have approached Olsten as an assemblage of localities or fields, each one part of a larger interconnected structure. During the initial stages of my research my approach shifted from doing continuous participant observation in the premises of temp agencies in Stockholm, Leeds and Santa Clara, towards temporary visits and a focus on in-depth interviews and structured conversations. These offices have nevertheless functioned as a sort of base for booking interviews and meetings with the temps, and for participating in different kinds of company events. For the temps, too, these offices work as a base, through which they are booked out on assignments at client organizations, and to which they return every now and then for meetings, classes, or for administrative reasons.

Olsten Corporation is a translocal organization, where linkages between the subsidiaries are multiple and complex and made up of structural relations of ownership, authority, common visions and policies, reporting systems, common symbols and artefacts and more or less shared perspectives and knowledge. It can be seen as a 'translocality' in Appadurai's terms (1996: 192), which stresses the fact that the organization is made up of individuals, objects and perspectives on the move, and that it exists in some sense over and beyond a given geographical territory. Translocalities tend to be organizationally unstable and to provide relatively little in terms of a sense of 'community'. They are more like 'virtual neighbourhoods'. We can not expect informants to be continuously close by, but will have to follow in their footsteps between workplaces, conferences, meetings and events of various kinds.[4]

Defining the objects of study is a matter of construction and of movement and tracing within different settings. In the case of temping, the cultural phenomenon of flexible work can, by interlinking sites, people and ideas, thereby be given a tentative conceptual identity, as contingent and fluctuating as the field that defines it. By not sticking to a predefined notion of the ethnographic field, as congruent with the boundary of one workplace, but rather studying 'down, up, sideways, through', as it were (Hannerz 2006), I have been able to get some sense of how the practices of management, evaluation and training link up with retrospective notions of career planning, with the development of mobility scripts and with the learning of market discipline. This mode of constructing multi-sited fieldwork assisted me in suturing locations of cultural production that were not connected by obvious spatial boundaries. It allowed me to 'see' the temping zone as a fragmented, discontinuous, yet interconnected field of cultural production and governance. Through my fieldwork, I have tried to follow the connections and threads among sites that together constitute the flexible temping field. As Marcus (1998: 90) puts it:

> Multi-sited research is designed around chains, paths, threads, conjunctions, or juxtapositions of locations in which the ethnographer establishes some form of literal, physical presence, which an explicit, posited logic of association or connection among sites that in fact defines the argument of the ethnography.

Moreover, research in the temping zone has involved what Wulff (2002) refers to as 'yo-yo fieldwork', a continuous movement back and forth between home and field. Rather than extended participant observation in a particular location, I maintained relations with the company over time by going back and forth between home, agency offices, the workplaces of temporary employees and other places. I have striven to attend the meetings, social events and other occasions that seemed relevant to the topic of my research in a broad sense. Yo-yo fieldwork has involved trying to stick with 'the logic of association' rather than 'being there' in a more stable sense. I have worked from the assumption that it is at the very crossroads of organizations, workplaces and ideas that we may understand what 'flexibility' in the temping world is all about (see also Garsten 2008).

Long-term participant observation, with dense and multi-layered relations, has generally been taken to indicate that the anthropologist has been fully accepted, has 'found her feet', and hence that the material gathered may be reliable and not too much influenced by the researcher's presence as an outsider. Fieldwork in the 'temping zone' has involved the experience of an 'inverted temporality' (Hannerz 1998), in which I have often found myself being more of an 'oldtimer' than my informants. Often I wondered: How much did I 'really' understand of the daily worklife of temps? How close did I get to the 'real' conditions, experiences, perspectives and imaginations of temps? These were questions that bothered me from time to time, and to which I returned during the analysis of my material. However, there were also instances when I thought to myself that the same questions would probably also be bugging anyone involved in fieldwork. The sincerity of many of my informants, the interest they took in our conversations, and the directness with which they responded to my questions left me with the confidence that my understanding of their world of work was reasonably close to theirs. In studying complex organization or powerful elites, Gusterson says, we may have 'to abandon, or at least subordinate, the research technique [participant observation, my insertion] that has defined anthropology as a discipline' in favour of multi-site fieldwork and more varied forms of relations with informants (1997: 116). One could characterize my relations with informants as 'polymorphous engagements' in Gusterson's terms. My relations with informants have varied greatly, some being short-term and defined by topicality only, some stretching over time and across places, with discussions ranging from the mundane and everyday to the core topic. This is also reflective of the field itself and its patterns of sociality, where episodic and discontinuous relations intermingle with long-term, cumulative relations. In response to anxieties related to a perceived loss of depth and intimacy in ethnographic research into dispersed and transient organizations, we should perhaps follow Marcus' suggestion that the quality of ethnography should be understood with reference to the anthropologist's relationship and connection with the object of study rather than by depth (Marcus 1998: 246). Along these lines of thinking, I believe my earlier experiences from doing fieldwork in the corporate world (see, for example, Garsten 1994, 1999) has equipped me with some knowledge as to the context of corporate activity, ways of thinking, tropes and metaphors in use, and the like.

Comaroff and Comarroff have pointed to the 'awkwardness' of an ethnography of scale, and pose the critical question:

> First, the aforementioned fact that almost everything which falls within the discursive purview of contemporary anthropology exists, in the phenomenological world, on a scale that does not yield easily to received anthropological theories or methods; and second, that our 'subjects' no longer inhabit social contexts for which we have a persuasive lexicon, not least because abstract nouns like society, community, culture, and class have all been called into question in this ever more neoliberal age (cf. Stoller 1997: 82), this age of the scare quote-around-everything, this age of ironic, iconic detachment. What, in the upshot, are we left with? A very stark question: Has ethnography become an impossibility? Have we finally reached its end? (Comaroff and Comaroff 2003: 152)

The Comaroffs believe not. Nor do I. From within their own field-work experiences they build a convincing argument around an 'anthropology-for-the present', one that dissolves the *a priori* breach between theory and method in the sense that the notion of the bounded ethnographic field in an evermore interconnected world had to be left behind, whilst the methodological priority of the locally bounded field still lingers on. This is also an anthropology of multiple dimensions that 'seeks to explain the manner in which the local and the translocal construct each other, producing at once difference and sameness, conjuncture and disjuncture' (2003: 172). Their argument is one in favour of tapping into flows of articulation, seeking out the points of interconnection, and mapping out the ways in which the 'local' as well as the 'local subject' is fashioned by forces beyond immediate reach.

It may well be that in studying global processes of social and cultural change, the trajectory of an idea such as 'flexibility' pro-vides the 'logic of association' and the cultural continuity that links up disparate organizations, workplaces, assignments and people (cf. Martin 1994, Marcus 1998: 92–93). 'Grounded ethnography' in complex and discontinuous fields may well have to be just as complex and seemingly discontinuous. It may ask more of us as ethnographers in terms of defining what actually makes up the field, what is really at stake in the field, where its boundaries are being drawn, and what the connections and threads between its sites are (cf. Ortner 1997, Moeran 2005). Grounded ethnography may involve meeting the informants where they are, going 'where the action is' – whether in Stockholm or some other locality. It means understanding the experiences of organizational actors, spatial and temporal, and exploring their local and translocal contexts. Mapping out the distinctive cultural and political terrain of the workplace vagabonds, and understanding their role in the global economy, has been a truly multi-site and yo-yo-like endeavour.

And so, I have been involved in tracing the linkages of work imaginings, trajectories and forms of governance – that which makes up the canvas of flexible work – across organizational, national and cultural boundaries. The story that emerges is one of complex and contradictory discourses and practices, of empowerment as well as exploitation, of 'responsibilization' as well as control, of negotiated and contested identities, careers and communities in the making. It is also a story of the creative agency of women and men who try to balance their own interests with those of large-scale organizations.

3
'Jumping Around': Translocal Movements

Ready to go

It is 8.10 a.m. on a Tuesday morning in November. The phone rings. As Susan is expecting a call, she quickly picks up. It's Lissie, her assignment coordinator at the Olsten Stockholm office. Lissie has found a new assignment for Susan. Is she interested? The assignment is with a telecommunications company located about ten kilometres outside of Stockholm, in Kista. According to the job description given by the client, the assignment seems to fit Susan's profile and skill level. The length of the assignment also seems to fit her availability. And Lissie also thinks Susan would fit in well overall, judging from what she knows about the company generally. What does Susan say?

Susan is happy about the phone call and the offer. It has been ten days since she quit her last assignment, and she has been waiting for something to turn up. The business area is perfect, it is exactly what she was aiming for. She thinks to herself that the task seems to be somewhat less challenging than what she had hoped for, but may on the other hand give her an inside view and open up other doors in the near future. The pay level is already set by her contract with the agency, so she need not worry about that (as temps in the UK or US would have to). The only thing that bothers her a bit is the distance between home and the worksite. She would have to spend one hour commuting morning and evening, since she lives on the other side of the city. However, turning down an assignment at this point would not be a good move, so she accepts it.

Susan notes down the name of the client organization, makes sure she got the address correctly, as well as the name of the contact person in the company, and finishes the call. Her working clothes are already prepared. As always before the first day of an assignment, she takes care to be prepared if and when the next assignment comes up. To facilitate the move between workplaces, she has created routines for herself that help speed up the process. Being prepared means having her clothes ready and a map at hand, since it is often the case that once the temp agency calls her, time is short. She calls these routines her 'mobility routines'.

Transorganizational moves

Temps move around a great deal. They quickly learn that temp work is associated with mobility and that each work location is a temporary one. Their patterns of movement vary, with some temps being assigned for months in a row to the same organization, and others changing organization on a weekly, or even daily, basis. But they share the continuous criss-crossing of organizational boundaries, which makes their moves transorganizational in character.

In the above example Lissie, the assignment coordinator, has already gone through a long work process of finding and following up on a lead, getting the job order and sourcing candidates before making the call to Susan. Susan's résumé has been read and evaluated, her previous assignments checked up, and her performance scrutinized. Managing the flow of people across organizations and through the agency is a complex and time-consuming job, and one that requires careful monitoring of candidate profiles as well as client needs. 'Essentially, we manage a vast network of organizations and people', one of the managers at Olsten explained to me. 'We need to invest considerable time and effort in handling this network in the most efficient way. And we need skilful and proactive coordinators to do it, people who know how to network.' And indeed, the transorganizational connections and moves involved in agency work to a large extent define and modify the daily work rounds and routines.

This chapter will focus on the mobility imperative that comes with temping and the kinds of expectations and experiences that this entails. The transorganizational moves of temps are an important aspect of their worklife and one that has to be learnt. The patterns of mobility of temps are deeply entangled with globalized labour markets and forms of capitalism, yet temps seldom occupy centre stage. They generally work behind the scenes in the theatre of corporate stardom, backstage as it were, but they play important roles in making the organizational wheels spin.

Move on, move on

We should keep in mind that the mobility of the temporary workforce is not something new. Historically, mobility has been a common trait among certain categories of temporary workers, such as travelling salesmen, lumberjacks and farm labourers. Throughout history, people have been forced to go where there are jobs. Moreover, there has historically been a tendency to regard the more mobile categories of workers as having 'no real profession' and being somewhat marginal to society, a point of view that still lingers today.[1]

Generally, the fixing of people and positions to workplaces was intertwined with the managerial control regimes that emerged with Fordist patterns of production. With industrial mass-production, work came increasingly to be organized into linear work sequencing, increased interdependencies of tasks, a moving assembly-line, and greater amounts of rigidity and regulation (see, for example, Meyer 1981, Littler 1982, Noon and Blyton 1997). Place came to be important here, in that it was primarily the product items that were to pass along the conveyor belt and hence move, whilst the worker was to stay in his place and perform a monotonous series of repetitive actions. The flow-line and the segmented work tasks were in a sense dependent on the immobility of the worker for the system of production to function.

The emphasis placed on immobility was not confined to mass-production plant work, however, but permeated a large part of the labour market, and not least the public sphere. Employees were expected to show loyalty to the employer, to stay put, and were also rewarded accordingly by the age of retirement. The gold watch and a decent pension were symbols of long and faithful duty, loyalty and perseverance. Likewise, work advancement was to be managed basically within existing organizational structures, and not across them.

Migratory workers posited a bad example for career-oriented professionals.

Also, the development of welfare states and social insurance systems meant that policies aimed at fixing people and positions, controlling movement and rewarding long-term commitment, were implemented. In a developed welfare society, 'workplace vagabonding' should be the exception, not the norm. This was the case in Sweden, where sanctions were introduced to penalize people who were caught on the move without a fixed abode and a steady occupation. An 'ideology of rootedness' was developed, which honoured those who stayed in one place, and who could be pinned down spatially, as well as organizationally.

With changing structures of production, organizational restructurings in the direction of 'lean production', the growth of the service industry, an emphasis on continuous or 'lifelong learning', and more volatile work contracts, contemporary labour markets are again being tailored to accommodate more mobility. The mobility of temporary employees is part and parcel of a larger societal change process, where new organizational constellations and market demands entail new ways of organizing work. The flexible employees of today are rather contemporary variations on a familiar theme, in which the processes of globalization and flexibilization, and new forms of regulation, give temping its particular characteristics. The relations between employees and employers, as well as those between workmates, change accordingly. The expectation of long-term relations and rewards, continuity and stability, is replaced by an awareness of such relations being of a temporary and more volatile character. There is, instead, a 'mobility imperative' connected to work in the global market economy.

What is particular to the flexible agency workers of today is the way job assignments are mediated between client, agency and employee for a profit, and patterns of mobility are determined through negotiation between the needs of the client organization and the managerial practice of the agency. This opens up a site for regulation and for valuation of the employee at the juncture of the interests and needs of the client and the agency. The patterns of mobility, the performance and the appearance of the employee are governed through a market-oriented logic of short-term gain.

For people working through temporary placement agencies spatial mobility is built into the very working arrangement. The temporary employee has to be willing to move between worksites at short notice, and hence to shift between different corporate contexts and clients. Temps are in some ways boundary-breakers, continuously crossing the boundaries of organizational structures, cultures and systems of knowledge, as well as established views on career and work community. Whilst spatially more fixed forms of employment boundaries involving time, territory and technology generally confine people to linear career paths, a functional focus and a more narrow specialization, the work experiences of temps involve non-linear, cumulative and multifunctional experiences that make it difficult to foresee how one's skills will be deployed tomorrow.

In the eyes of the temp, mobility may mean not so much freedom of choice, autonomy and the right to self-assertion, as a forced mobility and uprooting, a relative lack of security, and an uncertain future career (cf. Bauman 1998b: 36). The temp's trajectory is to a great extent drawn and defined by client organizations in demand of labour, temp agencies pursuing business opportunities, and more specifically by assignment coordinators acting as mediators of work opportunities. The temping vagabond moves surreptitiously and has, in practice, little choice about his or her pattern of movement. Moreover, patterns of mobility are never fixed, except for the yo-yo-like swinging back and forth between the temp agency's premises and client organizations. The patterns of mobility that characterize temp work shape and limit the planning horizons as well as the career moves of the temp.[2]

Trajectories, pathways

Managing spatial mobility is a large part of everyday work routines. The temp agency is organized so as best to deal with movement, mediation and continuous changing of workplaces. The information from client organizations about vacancies to fill is organized into 'orders' and categorized according to type of client organization, type of position, skills requirements and other relevant criteria. Here, type of personality, gender, age, and the like may as well enter into the profile. The assignment coordinators tend to work in groups of five or six people and are organized into sections, roughly corresponding to their clients' industry type. They usually cater to around 30 temps each, depending on their experience and the length of assignments they handle. At their disposal, they have a set of 'infrastructural technologies' (Calhoun 1992): telephones, emails and faxes, and advanced administrative systems which enable them to carry out their tasks mostly from a distance. Throughout this process, the assignment coordinators are continuously interrupted by telephone calls, questions from colleagues, or other occurences. Barley and Kunda (2004) provide a rich account of the work of agency employees to get job orders and to locate candidates. They write 'Locating candidates with the right skills on short notice was just as vital for an agency's success as finding job openings'. Agencies often invest considerable resources in this process, and computerized databases for the management of information on contractors are vital for handling the flow of people. Continually 'generating traffic' and securing the 'flow of fresh blood' through the agency is vital to filling job orders (Barley and Kunda 2004: 119).[3]

The temporary employees themselves move from place to place, between workplaces, and between different units in the organizations. As a temporary employee, the rule is that you do not work in the office of the temp agency (although there are cases where the assignment is placed in the agency), but at a client organization.

There is a large variety of trajectories, or pathways, to be found among temps. There is the 'job hopper' (in Swedish, *hoppjerka*), who moves frequently across workplaces and rarely stays more than a few days on each assignment. The job hopper is typically a newcomer to the temping industry, one who is still learning the ropes and not experienced enough to take on the more demanding long-term assignments. My informants told me this was the usual way of starting out, the most demanding, but often also the more rewarding in that there was a lot of change built into it. The slightly derogatory notion of 'just a temp' was most often used in relation to the job hopper. Acting as a substitute, the job hopper was often an easy scapegoat as well as a welcome rescuer (as we will see in Chapter 6).

The more 'sedentary' temps were those on outsourced contracts, where the temp agency managed a whole set of functions for a client organization, such as customer service. In such instances, the temp could stay for an extended time, often a year or more, in the same workplace. He or she was then often surrounded by other temps from the same agency, who together made up an enclave of 'others' or 'strangers' in the hosting client organization. Patterns of mobility for these temps were less fragmented, yet they remained aware of the inherent mobility of their employment contract and their perspectives were geared to future movement.

The more usual pattern was somewhere in-between the job hopper and the more sedentary ones on longer stays, where mobility patterns could involve a few days with one client, a month with the next, six months with the third, two weeks with the fourth, and so on, the only fixed place being the temp agency, to which they always returned between assignments.

In Brian Hassett's manual for temporary employees, *The Temp Survival Guide: How to Prosper as an Economic Nomad of the Nineties*, the mobile character of work is given a promissory expression:

> *Temps are cool*
> Temps answer to no one. We're like the nomadic circus workers of the Wild West, the Woody Guthrie train hoppers, the woolly menace Dennis Hoppers, the secret spies who slip under cover of the night. People don't even know our names. We don't ever have to be anywhere, or do anything, and that's the way things are going to stay.
>
> Temping will expand the flight pattern of your migrations. No longer will you be walking the same road to the same factory to work with the same people until the lights go out. As an autonomous free human at the crest of the millennium, you're in a world of geographic freedom where laptops and cellphones are taking you places your grandparents couldn't even imagine. And now your skills are about to take you even further! (Hassett 1997: 4)

The freedom associated with flexible work is here redefined as a capacity for mobility. One's success in getting a job assignment and in securing a degree of continuity and development resides to a large extent in one's capacity to move to where the job is and, at best, in achieving a sense of control over one's pattern of mobility.

Translocal career movements

The concept of career has indeed been a key notion in twentieth-century Western societies. Often used as shorthand for work histories and patterns, it connotes continuity, coherence and social meaning for people. 'Careers' connect people to the labour market, employment and the wide society in ways that are (at best) both personally meaningful and beneficial to organizations and society at large. While there are many discussions around the concept, its shifting uses and drifting definitions, it is elastic enough to cover a variety of functions and contexts (for an interesting discussion, see Young and Collin 2000).

In a complex and shifting organizational world, driven by market need and client expectations, career takes on altered significance. The flexibilization of employment contracts challenges the idea of a steady and continuous path of career development. Professional continuity and sense of development have to be construed from a series of temporary and translocal projects, assignments and competencies, rather than from a long-term contract with a single employer. In order to understand its meaning for temporary employees, we need to broaden the use of the concept to highlight the ways in which 'workplace vagabonds' create meaning out of worklife experiences in an unfolding sequence of assignments, contracts and workplace settings.

For temps, the notion of career is increasingly disconnected from previous attachment to status, position and structure, to describe experiences of work across and beyond these. Career to a large extent becomes a post-facto rendering of one's work trajectory that does not always neatly correspond to the initial motives and reasons for entering the temping zone, as it were. To some extent, the notion of career has always depended on a retrospective glance at the unfolding of events. However, in the temporary employment business, this aspect is highlighted and brings to the fore the individual rendering of account, as well as the contingent conditions under which the construction of career takes place.

Careers have been described as becoming more 'fragmented', emphasizing contemporary worklife as discontinuous and frail, and as contributing to new divides in terms of contract conditions, pay, skills development opportunities and gender. For example, in a study of young adults in Bristol, Fenton and Dermott (2006) suggest that people's engagement with work is becoming more like a series of encounters than an enduring relationship, hence the notion of 'fragmented career'. A related notion is that of 'portfolio work' (see, for example, Cohen and Mallon 1999, Haunschild 2004). 'Portfolio' directs attention to the transition of professionals out of organizational employment and into more flexible forms of contracts and the concomitant need to develop a portfolio of transferable experiences and skills. The demise of the traditional hierarchical career, or a move towards what has generally been termed 'the boundary-less career' (Arthur and Rousseau 1996, Haunschild 2003) is widely acknowledged to be linked to a proliferation of more fluid and insecure contractual conditions and individual career choices. More broadly, conceptualizations of portfolio careers and fragmented careers also highlight that relations between individuals and organizations are becoming less based on expectations of mutual engagement and more on explicit and contract-based transactions of labour for compensation.

New and emerging notions of career have also been connected to subjectivity, self-disciplining techniques and governmentality. Grey (1994) suggests that the project of self-management has become a defining feature of contemporary subjectivity. The discursive and non-discursive practices of career, he argues, sets into motion a particular discipline as an aspect of this contemporary project of self-management. In this process, the pursuit of career has the potential to transform techniques of disciplinary power into adjuncts of these projects of the self. This linkage of self-disciplinary practices of control and mobilizations of career is a particular fruitful avenue for the exploration of new forms of surveillance and control in flexible labour markets. As we shall see in Chapter 5, 'auditability' (Power 1997) and subtle forms of control are crucial aspects of the world of temping.

All in all, then, traditional notions of career have less to say about the processes through which people's movements and stops in the flexible labour market work to fashion a meaningful understanding of one's worklife. While not wanting to leave the notion of career behind altogether, I suggest that the notion of 'trajectory' is better able to capture the process through which temporary employees move through the labour market, contribute to creating and changing work settings and organizations through their moves, and how their mindsets and actions are influenced by, as well as influence, the organizations in which they work. 'Career has essentially been oriented to the future, and related past and present to it', Collin writes (2000: 91). It has also been related to the locating of individuals in space that has entailed more of spatial continuity than temping can offer. The notion of trajectory provides us with a more pliable view of the unfolding and connected worlds of work in contemporary global capitalism. These trajectories are, as we shall see, also infused with notions of alertness and competition that rests on market-oriented perceptions of worklife and subjectivity.

Learning mobility

Many of the temps interviewed view the experience of mobility as rewarding. Moving between organizations and sectors gives them ample opportunity to learn how different organizations work and what it is like to work in different kinds of industries. Moving across departments gives them a broad overview of the organization, which often puts them in a favourable position when it comes to acquiring important information. In my interviews, I very rarely heard them speak of their work as involving 'deskilling'. On the contrary, most of them told me about opportunities for learning and for broadening their skills repertoire.

These new forms of spatial flexibility have the potential of making the very changing of workplaces appear relevant and valuable, since it entails opportunities for learning and hence enables employees to feel more skilled, knowledgeable, autonomous and self-directing. If one learns to handle the built-in mobility to one's advantage, one may come to see oneself as a 'better worker' and a 'better self', simultaneously helping the temp organization, the client organization and oneself in current and future work (cf. Garrick and Usher 2000).

Quite frequently, however, I also heard tales of routine, monotony and even boredom, as temps recounted the repetitive tasks they were assigned to do. For many of them, temping was clearly associated with doing the routine tasks that others in the client organization did not want to take on, and filling positions in which the employee could easily be substituted for by another temp. In such instances, mobility was clearly less connected to learning, and more to a taken-for-granted work feature one simply had to learn to cope with.

In the view of agency staff, temps constitute important information links between the client organization and the temp agency. They bring 'home' valuable information and knowledge about the ways of client organizations and the workings of particular work routines, processes or technologies. They bring experience, new sales leads and – not to be forgotten – income and profit. Agency staff can in this way stay abreast of the development in the field, accommodate the client's demands more easily and foresee future contract opportunities. This is why temps are often talked about as 'ambassadors' of the temp agency, representing the agency in a professional and attractive manner at the client organization and scanning for future sales possibilities.

There are, however, some problematic aspects in this situation. For one thing, learning to embrace the mobility imperative invites an increased potential for surveillance and governance. It becomes not only a source of empowerment, but also a form of distanciated control, in which the worker herself is actively engaged. Zygmunt Bauman (1998a: 112) says of flexible labour:

> The pressure today is to dismantle the habits of permanent, round-the-clock, steady and regular work; what else may the slogan of 'flexible labour' mean? The strategy commended is to make the labourers *forget* [italics in original], not to learn, whatever the work ethic in the halcyon days of modern industry was meant to teach them. Labour can conceivably become truly 'flexible' only if present and prospective employees lose their trained habits of day-in-day-out work, daily shifts, a permanent workplace and steady workmates' company; only if they do not become habituated to any job, and most certainly only if they abstain from (or are prevented from) developing vocational attitudes to any job currently performed and give up the morbid inclination to fantasize about job-ownership rights and responsibilities.

As indicated by Bauman, mobility is something one learns. It requires that one learns to gear one's expectations towards change and movement, rather than towards stability and long-term stays. It requires as well that one develops habits and routines to support the mobile character of work. To be able to 'jump around' in a successful way, one has to be willing to adapt to different workplace cultures and to different social environments, to different expectations and demands of client organizations. Whilst one needs to have a will of one's own, one should also show versatility in engaging in the different tasks that may appear. In other words, one has to be 'flexible'.

Part of 'being flexible' is thus related to the spatiality of temporary agency work. As a temp, you are expected to meet new people for each assignment, to work with people you have never worked with before, and to find your feet in a variety of different organizational cultures. People who have temped for some time learn to feel relaxed about the continuous changing of social context, and develop what they call a 'social competence' for dealing with new social environments. Sandra, who works for Olsten in Santa Clara, tells me she used to be quite nervous about changing workplace, but having temped for a year, she hardly gets nervous any more, just a bit alert. She also knows that certain topics of small talk are best avoided. If not, you risk getting into internal politics or gossiping, which might ruin your position if you happen to step on the wrong toes. Similarly, Mats, who works for Olsten in Stockholm, reports he takes care not to engage in any personal or intimate conversations with workmates in the client organization, since it may turn out to your disadvantage. He says, 'And, there is really no point in it, since you will soon move on to a new assignment'. Just as important are *un*learning certain expectations and demands in relation to work.

Olsten encourages and creates flexibility in relation to space in their employees. In a handbook for temporary employees, *Temping, The Insider's Guide* (Rogers 1996: 20), it is suggested that mobility may be experienced as a great strain, but it is nevertheless something you have to be able to deal with in order not to feel like 'the perennial outsider':

> Since you are constantly changing worksites, you may not have the opportunity to get acquainted with co-workers or feel part of a team. You may have to trade the personal nature of permanent employment for the freedom and flexibility of temporary employment. If you need to feel like you belong, or you get possessive, then temping can be very hard emotionally.[4]

Learning to deal with spatial discontinuity on the job also entails changing one's perspectives and expectations of what the job can offer socially. Monica, at the Stockholm office, says:

> I would like to have a regular job, go to the same workplace every day, where I meet the same people. That's what I want to do. It's so disturbing knowing that you will not stay with the people you

have started to get to know. Even if you don't always get along with everyone, I'd still like to belong to one workplace, so to speak. But for now, this is the way it is. I think I learn a great deal by having to change places all the time. At least all my shyness is gone and I have much higher self-esteem than when I first started this job.

Something one has to unlearn is thus expecting work to provide a basis for the development of a sense of belonging and of permanency. Early on in the interviews, temps told me that they quickly figured out that they were not to look for friendship or long-term relations at the client organization. Rather, the kinds of job they performed were not supposed to be dependent on collegiality or local knowledge, but on their own capacity to perform, regardless of place and context.

Moving across organizational structures could also be seen to place the temps at a distance from gossiping and politics, which were regarded as taking time and energy away from the actual work. 'Boundary breaking makes you feel free', as one temp put it. 'I feel like I am on top of internal gossiping and politics, and that there are no such strings attached to my job.' Staying out of internal small talk and politics was most often a choice on the part of temps. In fact, a number of the temps stated that they valued exactly this aspect of temping, having had enough of the social density of work in their previous work experiences.

The positive side of this position is that temps over time come to function as organizational sounding-boards, strategically positioned to acquire a wide range of information. Lotta, employed through Olsten in Stockholm, gives voice to the intermediary aspect of temporary reception work:

To be a temp, you should be able to provide good service and to help out. And you have to have an interest in people. Because the reception, where I work, is not just a reception. It's the social point of connection for the entire company. And we are sounding boards for everything. And especially if you have been with the company for a longer time…. And what is said in the reception should stay there. You get to hear a lot. Because it's like a neutral zone where people can unburden their hearts…. And you develop an eye for people. How are they feeling? How do they work?

Possible conflicts. Lots of things like that. And if you are interested in people it can be quite rewarding, too.

Here, the notion of 'the stranger' may alert us to the particular
position of the temp in the client organization; she is *in* the place but
not *of* it. The stranger is, in essence, the potential wanderer, Simmel
writes, 'although he has not moved on, he has not quite overcome
the freedom of coming and going' (1959: 402). This liminal position
allows people to engage more freely with the temp, since she has no
long-term commitments, nor is she drawn into networks of loyalty
and interest. Unburdening your heart to a temp is perceived as incon-
sequential, since her position in the organization is marginal and
weak. Somewhat paradoxically, thus, it is precisely this liminal position of being 'betwixt and between' organizational structures that
provides the temps with ample opportunities for learning through
acting the part of the boundary-breaker (see also Garsten 1999).

Scripted mobility

Much of organizational life is carefully scripted; so also in the
temping industry. Temps learn to play their work roles by prescribed
rules of conduct in organizationally approved dress codes and display the right attitude to work. The 'temping scene' is in many ways
a carefully scripted performance of theatrical illusions, that play out
the processes of globalization, the pervasiveness of market ideology,
and the specific requirements of temps.

The current shift towards market-based forms of employment and
an entrepreneurial work ethic involves new ways of securing loyalty
and commitment and new forms of scripting that change both the
substance and the style of emotional labour (see Kunda and Van
Maanen 1999).[5]

Being continuously on the move, with little shared local knowledge and norms to rely on, temps learn scripts to provide a degree of
predictability to otherwise unpredictable situations. They create
their own scripts, or 'mobility routines', to deal with mobility, such
as preparing the work outfit, having city maps readily at hand, finding the best way to calculate the quickest transportation and figur-
ing out the time it takes to get from A to B. The more experienced
you are, the less time you have to spend getting ready before a new

assignment. Being well prepared becomes part of the job. Marie, at Olsten in Stockholm, tells me about the first period of temporary work and the routines she developed to handle the mobility:

> You learn. Yes, you learn a great deal about how to deal with moving from one assignment to another. When I did short-term assignments, I had to be more or less ready by 7 a.m. They [the agency, my insertion] might call me between 7 and 10 a.m. and send me somewhere. So I tried to get up in time, around 6 a.m. to get going, because I learnt that if I didn't, the day was just spoilt, more or less. I gradually came to like getting up that early, to have my shower, have breakfast in peace and wait. Then they might not call until 9 or 10 a.m. That was heavy. You sat there, basically, all ready to go, and nothing happened. That was tough. ... But when you got the assignment it was awfully stressful anyway. You had to run for the bus or the metro, check up on the best way to get there. And when you sat on the bus or the subway, you were thinking, 'What if I don't find it! What if I take the wrong street and then I have to run and I may not find the place!' I don't know. ... The worst thing that could happen was that I'd miss the bus or something and then I'd get really upset, and they would be waiting for me at the client's and then they would call the agency. I mean, they would wait for me, but then I would be so upset that I might do something wrong once I started the assignment. That's what I thought.

Temp agencies also provide scripts for their temporary employees. Along with the written information handed over to new recruits at Olsten in Stockholm is a sheet of paper headed 'Things to remember while working at Olsten'. These tips state that you should:

- Be prepared – when we call you should be ready to go
- Leave home in time
- Introduce yourself at the client's
- Show respect
- Keep a low profile in the beginning of a new assignment
- Don't take on the customer's bad habits
- Be curious and take initiative
- Always be on time

- Tell your contact person at Olsten about your strengths, weak-nesses, goals and visions

More thorough information on the company and its goals and practices is given in a folder called 'A job to love' ('Ett jobb att älska', my translation). Along with the corporate vision and more general information, a number of concrete guidelines as to how to fill in your timesheet, during what hours to be on standby for a new assign-ment, how to call in sick, etc., are given. A couple of timesheets and envelopes are included, as well as an Olsten pin to wear at work.

Similar information and scripts are provided by the agencies in Leeds and Santa Clara. As part of the 'framing' of a new temp, the assignment coordinators give them detailed and clear instructions on how to manage flexibility and the mobility that comes with it. Pamela, one of the assignment coordinators in Santa Clara, says:

> Since we don't see our temps during the day or the week, we have to make sure they get all the instructions and advice beforehand. We just can't, you know, check up on them, visually, I mean. But we tell them they need to prepare their clothes the day before, to make sure they have proper clothes that fit with any assignment, to have a map at hand, a notebook to note down the address, and things like that. If they don't prepare, they may get stressed out, and that's not a very good beginning. We don't want that to happen.

Indeed, getting stressed out happens easily. This is also something the authors of self-help books for the temping industry have picked up on:

> Meeting new people and getting involved in new situations can be exciting and exhilarating. It can also be stressful. Even if you're a seasoned temp and you've had hundreds of first days, they can still produce anxiety. If you've had some notice, figure out what you're going to wear the night before the assignment starts, so you don't have to worry about it in the morning, and get a good night's sleep. I try to feel confident about my ability. If I'm sure I can do the job, that makes me feel better; it also makes the people I am about to meet feel better. When I'm going into a situation where my skills have become a little rusty (especially if I've told my

personnel coordinator that I'm an expert at something I haven't done in two years), I pull out a book the night before and go over the important points of, let's say, a software program.

Besides being well groomed, try to get to the assignment at least fifteen minutes before you're supposed to start work so that you can familiarize yourself with the environment and equipment. (Rogers 1996: 112)

As Tilly (1999: 55) puts it, 'Scripts alone promote uniformity, knowledge alone promotes flexibility – and their combination promotes flexibility within established limits'. Temporary staffing agencies and client organizations typically provide enough scripts so that relations have broadly predictable rhythms and outcomes but also enough local knowledge so that temps, agency staff and client employees can improvise in the face of unexpected events. Scripts and local knowledge, rather than being contrasted with each other, are necessarily intertwined (Stinchcombe 1990). The homogenization of corporate vocabularies and terminologies in itself provides a global 'script' with which to approach particular local contexts with a degree of predictability and security. Being familiar with the hot concepts, the favoured terms and the technical terms facilitates movement between particular local contexts. Such scripting bestows the possibility of shared assumptions and eases communication within the context of a dislocation of work time and work place (Tilly 1999).

It is adeptness in this script – knowing one's lines, knowing the plot, knowing one's role – that constitutes a transferable skill, rather than the knowledge of techniques to which the language notionally refers. But, in addition, the acquisition of a capacity for 'corporate-speak' represents a form of predictability which is then a basis for trust. Temps are instructed to learn the business priorities, the vocabulary and the right expressions where they are. 'Corporate-speak' establishes not just a common language but a common set of understandings of the world (and in this sense is a discourse rather than a language). And such discourse has the capacity to construct subject positions. For example, the script of 'flexible adaptation' – that temps must serve client and agency needs – provides a communicative and normative framework and a potentially valuable identity. Scripting facilitates, as well as governs, the discontinuous and translocal work performance of temps. In a sense, temps delegate to a script the ability to attribute roles and to delegate actions to them. By adapting flexibly to the requirements of local work settings, they retain a degree of freedom to modify the script, whilst constantly monitoring the relation between the scripting rules and their fulfilling of the script (cf. Latour 1993).

Transferable selves

Transferable skills are often thought of in terms of their capacity to be used in different contexts without losing their value. But as we have argued elsewhere (Grey and Garsten 2001), transferability, and flexibility, can be read not simply in terms of the possession of a skills bundle but as attributes of the self. Olsten agencies will have hundreds, if not thousands, of temps on their books at any one time and the extent to which agency staff knows the temps personally is limited. On the other hand, they know a good deal about the requirements of client organizations, at least where these are regular clients, and will seek to ensure that particularly difficult jobs or clients are dealt with by 'good temps'. Good temps, unlike the mass of the temping staff, will be known to agency staff, who will go to some lengths to keep them on the agency's books. The attributes of a good temp are often not so much skills as the capacity to fit in with whatever organization they are assigned to. 'Basically, what we need are people who can meet the requirements of any one client, who can deal professionally with the difficult ones and who are independent enough to manage on their own', one of the senior managers in Stockholm explained. Thus, what is at stake is the transferable self, rather than transferable skills. A person who can be relied on (by both agency and client) to perform in a predictable way (to fit in, adapt, do a professional job) is a good temp. This is also another way of saying that trust is something that needs to be achieved (Grey and Garsten 2001). Symptomatically, Olsten staff in Stockholm sometimes refer to successful temps as 'chameleons', with a capacity to adapt effortlessly to the needs of the customer.

> Amanda told me what it takes to be a good temp: Education is not the most important. It really isn't. But you need to be open to ideas, impressions. Attentive. That's very important. That you overhear what they are talking about in the background. That

they might be saying 'Ugh, this coffee is bitter' and bla bla bla. You hear it and you happen to be walking by coincidentally, and you say, 'Could I make you some fresh coffee?' To just be ready. Take the opportunity. And that you are flexible. You absolutely need to be. You can't say: 'I am doing the invoicing. It's not my job to take messages.' You need to be flexible all the time. But not flexible to the extent that you agree to their terms all the time.

From the perspective of the temp there are also various understandings of what constitutes a 'good job'. Although this will partly be an issue of 'personality', more interestingly the temps report that assignments with large companies and companies that regularly use temps (which may or may not be the same) are good jobs to be on. In the former case, it was because large companies were relatively predictable in how they behaved and the tasks asked of the temp. In the latter case, because the expectations of what could reasonably be asked of the temp were realistic.

Fran, with two years' experience of temping with Olsten in Santa Clara, expresses her thoughts about what constitutes a 'good job':

The company needs to be organized before the temp arrives. You can't invite a temporary employee into a situation where there's no system. Because you will be wasting your money training them when you're thinking all the time: 'If only I'd organized before they arrived I wouldn't be spending two days having to do this'. And the temp is not doing anything in that time! The company needs to be professional about the whole relation to temporary employment. That's a problem, because I think there are a lot of companies who aren't. They're in a mess anyway and they usually call the temp agency because they need employees quickly. And they want dependable people, a dependable workforce ... and that's not what a temp agency is always good for because you get people who ... don't really wanna think much. They just wanna come in. Do the job and leave. And if you're not structured when they arrive ... that's that. Their arrival is not gonna help.

Office Angels also facilitates the introduction into a new assignment by providing the client with a 'Handover briefing form'. This is designed to make the 'setting in' process smoother by providing some basic information for the first days of a new assignment. On the front cover, there is a request from the agency addressed to the client:' In order to assist the Office Angels' replacement to settle in, it would be helpful if this Briefing could be completed and left for her/him in a prominent place. Thank you!'

To fill in are: information of the company's main activity; the work of the department; names and titles of people the temp will be working with; where to find stationery, franking equipment; coffee/tea facilities, and the like; notes about the filing system and the correspondence distribution; dress code, smoking restrictions, office technology, and so on.

So the good job, like the good temp, turns out to be bound up with the reliability and trustworthiness of each. Interestingly, these two notions – the good job and good temp – have a tendency to self-fulfilling effects: agencies wish to keep good temps on their books for use in their most valued clients and will seek to accommodate the temp's desires. The temp prefers to go to a good job, and in such jobs it is easier to be seen as a good temp because these are the large, predictable organizations that habitually use temps. And, of course, it is such clients who are most valued by the agencies. The lynchpin of this set of relations is the trust generated between the different parties involved, such that the most impermanent types of employment are rendered at least relatively predictable. The discontinuity of space and time is thus partly compensated for by a set of scripting routines and a mutual degree of trust (see also Grey and Garsten 2001).

Thus a standardized set of vocabulary, a set of scripts, together with an attitude of preparedness and a set of transposable skills, provide a global 'grammar' which offers a basis for predictability within particular local settings. At the same time, certain organizational and business-related norms, built around notions of professionalism and flexibility, and an ethic of customer service, offer the basis of predictability which is not organizationally specific but which creates the subject position of the 'good temp', that render the person potentially controlled and controllable, predictable, and hence trustworthy (Grey and Garsten 2001).

In this way, the temporary worker, whilst engaged in an individual project of navigating changing organizational landscapes, is able to draw upon and reproduce values that exist beyond a single organizational setting. On entering such a local setting, she has a basis for connecting with wider meaning structures through her own understanding of professionalism, whilst also deploying the global knowledge structures of administrative temping.

Local horizons, translocal cultures

As Clegg et al. (2005: 180) have it, 'Organization work is a ceaseless round of activity. Most organizational members are in the middle of organizational chains whose links are not always clear.' This goes as well for temps in their organization work. Whilst they are clearly in the midst of organizational chains, they may not be interested in, or have access to, the larger organizational picture.

The built-in geographical mobility and the transient character of agency work influence the perspectives of the temps on the corporate structures they work within. Their work experiences and relations with colleagues and clients provide them with views, knowledge and perspectives beyond the local workplace. However, they are a far cry from the cosmopolitans of the worlds of diplomacy, executive business or academia, whose moves often stretch much further across national, cultural and social boundaries (Hannerz 1992: 252–253). The horizons of temps are often much more restricted, in so far as they move in local territory, between different organizations. There is a striking lack of awareness among the temporary agency workers of the global organizational structures of which they are a part. The episodic and transient character of their involvement with other temps and with agency staff also encourages a local and individualized perspective, and does not do much to foster an interest in exploring the wider organizational, economic or cultural networks in which they are enmeshed.

Very few of the temps I interviewed in Sweden and the UK actually knew that they worked for an American company, whose headquarters were located in Long Island, USA. Only a handful of my informants knew the location of the headquarters and that it had been run as a family firm for some time. They were hardly aware of the organizational structure, or of the management structure of the agency. When asked about the history of the company, few, if any, could tell me about it. Most of them did know that it had a global spread of some significance, but few could tell me about the locations, apart from the US. None of them had thought about working for Olsten in another region or country. In Hannerz' (1990) terms, Olsten temps are 'locals' – I would suggest 'mobile locals' – with circuits of mobility that are restricted to a regional business area. To them, the global workings of the enterprise are either hidden from view or irrelevant.

The limited outlook on the wider organizational structures should not conceal the fact that temps do often develop translocal perspectives that cut across client organizations and regional market sectors. It may even be argued that it is part of their job to gather knowledge about, and relate to, the core business of client organizations and their organizational and cultural characteristics. The translocal perspectives that temps develop are, however, dependent on the relations they establish with their contacts in the client organizations. By 'jumping around' they stand a good chance of developing their translocal perspectives over time.

Despite the limited global scope of their perspectives, temps are deeply drawn into global patterns of capitalism and labour market relations. Temps in general constitute an invisible category of corporate workers. They are the intermediaries that connect and interlink organizations, the fuel that makes the market spin, yet their presence is hardly noticed. Nor do they themselves have easy access to the structures of which they are a part. The kind of transboundary mobility we are engaging with here is a significant part of globalized labour markets, yet not easily discernible. It is the backstage of corporate stardom and visibility, the mundane everyday task of muddling through and of making organizations tick.

Conclusion: Embracing the mobility imperative

In this chapter, we have seen how flexible work entails continuous mobility across worksites and organizations. Being 'on the move' is built into the very idea of flexible, temporary work. From a distance, the migratory patterns that appear place the temporary agency at the very centre of the nexus. The moves of temps form a yo-yo movement between agency and client organizations. Up close, the everyday lives of temps entail being prepared to move, creating ways to deal with movement, by way of adjusting perspectives and expectations and using scripts to facilitate for themselves.

Mobility, more than being expected, is stipulated. Without the readiness to move, there would be no market for temporary agencies. Hence, movement is not undertaken freely, but circumscribed and defined by the market; by client demands and agency norms. The market for temporary services constitutes, in the unfolding of everyday events, an arena for negotiations, for tension, for engagement or acceptance. For temps, apart from engaging in an agreed transaction between organizations, it is also a way of life, a large part of which is made up of learning to read market cues, dealing with new forms of control, and also learning to act as the responsible, reliable temp.

A readiness to move is, in other words, a prerequisite for being a successful temp, and for moving up the career ladder. Mobility is not just important in itself, but is interlinked with getting more interesting assignments, with one's future career prospects. Accepting the built-in mobility of work, and adapting to the migratory patterns as defined by the agency, is generally viewed as a way to gradually gain control of your work trajectory. Thus, one aspect of flexibility is the ability to respond adeptly and resourcefully to change in terms of shifting locations of work, and the change of context that goes along with this shift. Variety and change in workplace location impose their own demands and constraints, and these differ from the more fixed roles and organizational structures associated with regular office work and bureaucratic work in general.

The spatial distances separating temporary workers from agency staff and from other temps, combined with the temporal discontinuities (to be discussed in the next chapter), calls forth new strategies for control that differ from those in place in centralized workplaces and types of jobs with greater degrees of spatial continuity. Temporary work spans multiple locations and crosses organizational boundaries. It is made up of widely distributed worksites, and of translocal organizations. Consequently, notions of control have to rely on different means from those in workplaces where people are localized under one roof. The flexible mode of control, or regulation, takes place at a distance, and at the interfaces of organizations. Temps are subjugated to the normative demands and control mechanisms of both agency staff and client organization management, whose interests converge, so to speak, on the temporary employee. Embracing spatial mobility, being ready to move, is a first basic requirement. This entails embracing the understanding of flexibility as mobility, change and unrest. It also presupposes adopting an attitude of readiness. And being prepared alerts one to time, to the here and now of temping, to which we now turn our attention.

4

Just-in-Time: Temping Timelines and Time Tools

> Do not squander Time, for that is the stuff life is made of.
> Benjamin Franklin

In my office, I had for quite some time the following poster ad glued to the wall:

The 6 stages of dealing with an overwhelming work load.

Denial: Work load. What work load?
Avoidance: I think I have some vacation coming up.
Desperate reasoning: If work = mass × force, then if I decrease my mass...
Panic: I can't do it! I'm going to be fired!
Acceptance: O.K.
Logic: I'll call Olsten.

The easiest way to deal with an overwhelming work load is simply to call Olsten. Olsten provides business and government with innovative and effective staffing solutions.

We offer experienced personnel in the full range of skills, from clerical, assembly and office automation personnel to senior-level professionals and more. Whatever you need, Olsten will match the job with the perfect person. So next time, do the logical thing. Call your Olsten office or 1–800–WORK NOW (capitals in original).

The poster ad was a gift from one of the assignment coordinators in Santa Clara. It captures something of the sense of urgency one feels when time is simply not enough and work threatens to take over and cause serious ruptures in life.

Time is a significant factor in fashioning work relations and in shaping our experience of work. Having too little time, a common feeling in contemporary organizational life, can cause work-related unease, tension and stress. Having too much time at our disposal can easily turn into feelings of monotony or boredom. Our subjective experience of time colours every worklife and influences our relation to the work community.

Control over time has long been an essential aspect of the employer–employee relationship. In a number of ways, employers have over time sought to impose their definition of time and to tighten control systems around time utilization. Different regimes of control, each with their own problems and solutions, have succeeded each other in a continuous search for more efficient, more rational production systems and modes of utilizing workers' time. The ability to synchronize individual activities within a larger production process has been a key feature of industrial development.[1] The ability to measure time, to divide it into units, and to allocate and monitor tasks accordingly, was an important element in the growth of mass production. With more flexible production systems, use of information technology and new managerial techniques, the temporal patterns of work change as well. The 'just-in-time' logic is based on the premise that what makes economic sense, what is rational according to market demands, is also preferable. Through casualization, delayering, outsourcing or externalization (the terms are many!) organizations can contract and expand quickly, shedding or adding personnel (Sennett 2006: 49). Time can be cut into small fragments, into short assignments and quick placements. Short-term, contingent and casual contracts are now challenging long-term employment contracts as the desired goal and the posited norm. Some indication of the significance of time in organizing and understanding work is also conveyed by the variety of terms used to define different kinds of flexible work – temporary, casual, contingent, short-term, zero-hours, on-call arrangements and just-in-time employment.

For the temps, flexible work also means flexible time. Assignments come and go, hiring and firing games are played without much advance notice, and opportunities twinkle and disappear. Temps know that employment may not be limitless, stretching into an indefinite future, but that it may well be terminated before one wants it to be. Temporary flexible work caters to the immediate needs of the client organization, to rescue, fill in or smooth out workload cycles. The flexibility and agility that temps are learning has a clear temporal aspect to it, in that they learn to adapt to the time cycles of others. Hence, the temporal orientation of employees is coloured by a sense of immediacy, transiency and urgency. Work time is not the linear sequence of unfolding events that it has often been taken to be, but rather punctuated and fragmented in character.

To deal with and make the best of things in this shifting 'work-scape' (to paraphrase Appadurai's metaphorical inventory of 'scapes' emerging and confronting each other in processes of globalization, 1990), one has to show a certain agility and preparedness. This chapter will focus on how temporary employees deal with the transient character of their employment and the risks attached to it, and how they go about constructing a sense of continuity in the midst of contingency. We will see that learning to deal with the specific temporalities of temping is part of the job, so to speak, and also a way of aligning the temporary employee with the organizational and managerial expectations and demands.

The seductive power of the here and now

We may recall the marketing campaign with the slogan 'Work when you want, be free when you want', 'Work when you want, be with your kids when you want', mentioned in Chapter 2. Flexibility is here imagined as involving a space of freedom in which you can tailor time to your own wishes. This promissory aspect of temporary work is presented to candidates as a major advantage of temping. 'In what other areas of worklife could you have the same freedom to decide when you want to work and when to be free?' was a question often posed rhetorically to me when I interviewed assignment coordinators. This allure of free time, of fluid time and of controllable time works seductively to attract temporary employees and keep them attached to the business. Anna, in Santa Clara, explains to me:

> The best part of temping is actually the freedom. That I can, if I feel like it, just say 'No, I don't feel like doing this assignment. I don't have time for it now. Can you please call me next time there

is something interesting coming up?' But hey, it doesn't always work this way. But you know what I mean, I could, if I wanted to.

What is striking about the temporal orientation of the temping industry as a whole is the strong 'here-and-now' orientation. The organizational culture of Olsten is characterized by a here-and-now character in which the future, as well as the past, tends to dissolve. It is culture with little durability built into it (cf. Bauman 2000: chapter 3). In the words of Lash and Urry (1994: 243) 'instantaneous time' means that 'the future is dissolving into the present'. Since the patterns of mobility, the timing of work assignments and the duration of them are varied and fragmented, it is difficult to foresee and plan for the future. Fran, who works for Olsten in Santa Clara, has a pragmatic view of the discontinuous temporality of temping:

> When you come to a new assignment, a new company, you go in there thinking 'I'm just a temp, it doesn't really matter what they think of me, I'm gonna be gone by tomorrow', type of thing. I know there were some which I didn't really care too much about that were around me, but I just told myself; 'OK, it's just for two days and I'll be out of here and I don't have to stay here' (*laughter*). It's the temporary thing about it. I'll just do what they want me to and do it good so that they'll want me back if they're ever in need of it. I just feel like it's temporary.

The fluidity of time in temping makes the significance of the transferability of skills and of selves all the more acute. To be able to fill in the gaps and to replace someone on leave in a reliable and swift manner, one has to be able to transpose one's skills and experiences to other contexts at short notice. Working in different organizations requires the transferable capacity to solve problems at hand. This takes some qualities other than those linked to the foreseeable, repetitive rhythms of regular administrative work. A certain adeptness in improvising is required.

To some extent, we may understand the temporal dimension of flexible work as associated more with improvisation than with careful organizational design. As Ciborra has it, 'Globalization, with its related risks and widespread side effects stemming from large-scale activities and systems, makes the highly situated process of improvization a valued intervention. This activity is needed to fill the gaps of planning, cope with unexpected consequences, and, in general, face emergencies' (2004: 153).

Certain aspects of temping can be understood in terms of 'kairotic time' rather than linear time (Czarniawska 2004). While Chronos was the Greek god of time, Kairos was the god of right time, of proper time. Kairos jumps and slows down, omits long periods and remains in others. The sense of urgency, the fragmented and punctuated nature of much temping, suggests that linear time is often overshadowed by 'kairotic time'.

Fragmented time, shallow time

On my way to work one morning, at the university, I happened to overhear a conversation in the elevator between two young women, one of whom was obviously combining studies with temping work. Her friend asked her if she wanted to join her and a group of other students for an outing at the end of the week. They were going picknicking in the nearby park. The conversation continued:

Student-temp: You know, I'd love to join you, but I have this arrangement with Manpower. They might call me in the morning for a short-term assignment. It suits me fine since I need to study as well, you know. So I don't really know.

Student: But don't you know in advance when you will be working?

Student-temp: Mostly no. They can call me any time, and I have to be prepared for that. Can I let you now later if I'll join you or not?

Student: Yeah, sure.

Richard M. Rogers, in his book *Temping: The Insider's Guide*, makes it clear that '...no matter how long or short a temporary assignment lasts, a temporary job is just that – temporary' (1996: 13). He continues:

To handle this one must be prepared for the insecurity this entails.

No job security: Not that there's much job security anywhere these days, but temping would certainly rank at the bottom of the list if job security is your goal. There are no guarantees, no commitments, no written contracts. Jobs that are scheduled for three weeks may last a day. Conversely, jobs that were supposed to last a day may go on indefinitely. If you're looking for something absolutely certain, then temping would not be for you. Of course, as the saying goes, there's nothing certain but death and taxes (1996: 19).

Working on temporary or flexible contracts involves having to deal with the increased temporariness of employment. The very concept of temporary employment entails that the relationship between employer and employee is of a transient nature, and no strong expectations of a continuous relationship are attached to it. Their work is supplied 'just in time', as it were, and the temporary employee needs to be accessible and prepared to take on a new assignment at short notice. In the words of Keri, in Santa Clara:

> Even people who you know you're smarter than, and whose job you can do twice as fast, they will turn around at you and look like they were saying: 'Oh, you're just a temp'. ... And if someone finds out you're a temp they don't treat you with the same respect. That kind of annoys me. And also, you know, I don't know what I'm gonna be doing from day to day and I'm afraid one day Tony [the manager at the client's] is just gonna say: 'We don't need you any more'. You know. Which I know probably isn't gonna happen, I really hope, until I get another job, but it's just the insecurity of knowing your job is not permanent. So that kind of stinks.

Many of my informants tell about catering to this perceived need of urgent replacement and assistance. Often, they say, they are more efficient and better equipped, both in terms of their attitude and their skills sets, to do the job faster and more efficiently than the 'regulars'. And since they are continuously evaluated, they also carry with them the knowledge that time efficiency enters into the judgement of their performance. Sometimes, they say, this stirs the competitive edge in the department, as the regulars are made aware of their own pace and achievement, and it can at times, cause irritation towards the temp. Marika, at Olsten in Stockholm, expresses the frustration of having to refrain from changing things around too much in order not to cause irritation among her workmates: 'In some places you think it's so incredibly inefficient and you want to, like, change everything around, so that that things would run more smoothly. Like they did at this other place I was at yesterday. But you can't just do that.'

While all organizations hold implicit as well as explicit assumptions about time, it is a general trait of so-called innovative and dynamic organizations to look to the future. An orientation towards the future is generally believed to encourage learning and creativity. The temporary staffing industry is, however, more clearly geared to solving the immediate problems of the here and now of other organizations. To dive too deeply into any one problem risks being poor use of time, since an assignment may end as quickly as it started. As stated in Chapter 3, the temp who can move on is more attuned to the instabilities in the flexible labour market. These tendencies risk contributing to a hollowing-out of the very learning that is envisaged as so valuable in temping. The pressures to produce results and fulfil the task quickly are at times too intense to cultivate a stimulating learning context. The workplace time–anxiety dynamic causes the temp to skim across a wide variety of sets of knowledge, rather than to engage deeply in any one of them. Jackie Krasas Rogers (1995: 146–148) argues that the temporarily fragmented nature of temping alienates the workers from the products of their work as well as from the work process as such. In her view, the temporary nature of the work deprives the temporary worker of even the most limited realization of the finished product of her work. This happens even on long-term assignments, because once the work is finished, the temporary moves on to another assignment. Seldom do temps complete subsequent stages of a project, which would provide them with a sense of continuity.

We can here understand how the use of a flexible workforce contributes not only to the positive development of a company's learning curve, but also to the growth of what is commonly called 'organizational amnesia'.

Balancing plural time perspectives

Temporary work, involving responsiveness to the production needs of client organizations, a continuous readiness for change, and movements between worksites, implies that there is not one time perspective, but many. It is perhaps the diversity of time schedules, rather than the unity of them, that is characteristic of the temping industry. Whilst management at the temporary staffing agency may have one understanding of time, management at the client organization may have another one. Both these perspectives may, and often do, differ from that of the temporary employee. Temporary agency staff often looks at the length of assignment as the focal point. Is the assignment a short-term one or a long-term one? Is it an outsourcing project, requiring a different kind of planning procedure? Is the client organization one that is likely to become a long-term and hence important account? The temporal perspectives of agency staff tend to be of linear sequences of time that are organized into different units. Their job is to find the suitable candidate for the one unit. The perspective of client organizations tends to be one of urgency and immediate need. True, vacancies and replacements can, and often are, planned. The outsourcing of a department or service also entails a long planning process. But more often, in my interviews, clients have talked about the urgent needs that temp agencies cater to. Temp agencies can do the job they themselves do not have the time for: advertise the opening, screen for candidates, evaluate them and guarantee their performance – or have them replaced. Temp agencies smooth out cycles and provide the elasticity they need.

For temps, flexible work implies learning to juggle unforeseeable temporal rhythms. To begin with, there is the difference between one's actual contract with the temp agency which implies a different and longer temporal perspective than that of the single assignment. As indicated before, temps in Sweden are usually employed on a regular basis through the temp agency. Hence, they keep track not only of the different temporalities of assignments, but also of their relation to the agency as employer. Temps in Santa Clara and Leeds may have relations with two or more agencies at the same time and thus have two or more temporalities to handle. Their employment contract with the agency is often of a shorter duration and a more fragile character than in Sweden, but does not necessarily correspond to a single assignment, either. There is thus a multitude of different durations and rhythms to keep in mind.

As for the assignments, they are sometimes prepared days in advance and there is a long-term horizon to go with them. At other times, jobs are offered the very same morning, requiring quick adaptation to a new place and new people. Marika expresses how she feels when trying to accommodate the urgent needs of the client:

> When I was going to a new assignment I used to be so worried I wouldn't get there in time. Then when I got there, they would say 'Where have you been?' And then I thought: 'Oh, well, now I'm in trouble!' Because they must have heard when they called in [to Olsten, my insertion] that it would take me an hour to get there. I mean even if Olsten promises, I may not be able to keep that promise. I mean, I live in the southern suburbs and I may have to be in the north for a job. It may take that long, and there's nothing I can do about it. And I don't know what they might have said at Olsten. 'She can do this and that, and she will be with you at 9 o'clock,' or something. And then they call me at 8.30 and it takes me one hour to get to this place! There's nothing I can do about it.

There is a sense in which flexible work can provide the freedom for people to carve out their niches and to make use of time in the way they themselves prefer. As we saw in Chapter 2, temps come to the temping industry with different motivations and expectations, some of which suggest they expect to tailor working time to their own needs. And some do. As they learn the 'tricks of the trade' they become more confident in asserting their own limits and their own preferences. As one manager at a client organization explained to me: 'It's getting harder and harder to find the temp who can come in and do the short-term project for us. They all want long-term assignments now.' For others, temping risks are becoming what Hochschild refers to as a 'temporal prison' (1997: 242). The amount of adaptation needed is too great for them to be able to carve out their own space.

The different perceptions of actors reflect different rationalities (cf. Noon and Blyton 1997: 55–76) where the organizational perspectives of client and agency stress the importance of regularity for the coordination of different time schedules and the importance of maximizing the productive use of working time. On the other hand, there is also a temps' perspective, seeking to deal with and mitigate the fragmented nature of work. These perspectives exist in a context of mutual influence, so that the 'time regime' defined by the organizational demands is, in part, balanced by what the temporary employees can accept.

Time tools

> The right person, in the right place, at the right time
> – to the right price
>
> > (Olsten postcard ad)

'Time management' has become a ubiquitous feature of organizational life, and so also in the temping industry. In order to be 'responsible' and 'reliable' temps are expected to learn to manage time so that they can deal with shifting assignments and tasks. A look at some of the tools and techniques through which this can be done gives an idea of the place of time management in the world of temping.

As indicated already, the telephone is an important tool for getting information on the new assignment and for keeping in touch with the agency. Likewise, temps are encouraged to carry cell phones and to make sure they have an email account so that the agency can reach them easily. A daily planner is also essential to map out time and keep things in order. And, as seen in Chapter 3, a map is essential to speed up the process of locating the client organization and the best and most time-efficient way to get there.

One of the more important tools is, of course, the timesheet that each temp has to fill in every day during assignments. It is handed over early in the recruitment process and the assignment coordinator then explains how it should be filled in. The timesheet is a crucial document, in that it details the number of hours worked, provides the basis for invoicing the client, and the salary of the employee. Tampering with the timesheet is a seriously regarded misdemeanour, and one that could result in the contract with the agency ending. The form provides tables in which the temp fills in location of temp agency, district, employment number, name, week number, effective work time, overtime, any sick leave taken, and so on. On a weekly basis, this is then sent to the agency coordinator.

The use of these time tools is encouraged by the temp agency as part of the process of facilitating a successful and smooth temping career, or trajectory.[2] And these time tools do often come in handy. But this should not blind us to the fact that they also work as disciplinary technologies that serve not only to monitor and calculate the value of the temp's effective work, as in the case of the timesheet, but also to manage the temp workforce from a distance. The significance of the timesheet as a disciplinary tool is evident in the newsletters that Olsten distributes to all their temporaries. The front cover of one issue of the Office Angels Newsletter asks: 'Are *you* a timesheet sinner!?'

The news item then continued:

> 7 TEMPS FAILED TO ENSURE THEIR TIMESHEETS ARRIVED ON TIME LAST WEEK! TUT, TUT.
>
> IT IS VITAL THAT YOU STICK TO THE TIMESHEET DEADLINE EVERY WEEK. PLEASE SEND US YOUR TIMESHEET ON FRIDAYS. MONDAY 10.00 A.M. IS THE CUT-OFF TIME TO BE PAID BY FRIDAYS. THANK YOU FOR YOUR COOPERATION! (underlining and capital letters in original)

In the same issue, one could also read that by leaving one's timesheet in time, one could qualify for a surprise gift:

> EVERY WEEK, ONE TEMP WINS A SURPRISE GIFT!
>
> WE WILL AWARD A PRIZE TO A TEMPORARY WORKER WHO HAS COMPLETED A FULL WEEK'S WORK WITH NO SICKNESS OR LATES! TO QUALIFY, MAKE SURE YOUR TIMESHEET ARRIVES BY 8.30 MONDAY MORNING! CONGRATULATIONS TO OUR LATEST WINNERS: SIMON OLIVER AND VICTORIA GREYSON! [names have been changed]

In the above, we see that 'lates', sick leaves and late arrivals of timesheets are best avoided. Punctuality and reliability are also things that are made part of the evaluation procedure after each assignment, as will be shown in Chapter 5. Clearly then, an alertness to the value of time discipline and time management, and a serious attitude to the many time tools available, are part of the temping job.

Being attentive to the temporal dimension, being prepared, is also fostered by rewards. Office Angels in Leeds nominate temps monthly for the *Temp of the Month Award*. In their newsletter (5 September 1997), the upcoming challenge was announced:

> DO YOU HAVE WHAT IT TAKES TO BE A TEMP OF THE MONTH?

Every month we get together to make a tough decision – WHO SHOULD BE TEMP OF THE MONTH? We look for qualities such as flexibility, loyalty, dedication or dropping everything at the last minute to take on an urgent booking. The feedback and praise from our clients is currently outstanding (thank you!) and they get the chance to nominate you too. (underlining and capital letters in original)

Time discipline is thus integral to flexible work. Externally imposed technologies here work side by side with an internalized self-discipline. While the factory system of the Fordist production system required 'regularity and steady intensity in place of irregular spurts of work' (Pollard 1965: 213), flexible work has instead to be regulated by the inculcation of norms, the use of tools and scripts, and by 'responsibilization' (cf. Grey 1997). To some extent, though, the logic of punishment still remains. Temps who are late to their first assignment or, worse, who fail to show up at all, are strongly reprimanded or, in the latter case, lose their contract with the agency.

Time reflexivity

Flexible forms of work bring forth a more reflexive relation to time and to one's identity as a temp. Time becomes a central theme for the flexibly employed, for the 'time pioneers', as Hörning et al. (1995) call them. Flexible work influences how people create meaning in their worklife, since the particular spatial and temporal patterns force them to reflect on how they deal with and engage with time and sets into motion different strategies for dealing with the fragmented character of work. The transformation of temporal and spatial patterns propels temps away from established precepts and practices of work. The temporal dimension also symbolizes a lifestyle that is different from the more conventional – a lifestyle less subordinated to the homogenizing demands of industrial society and that promises to make possible new ways of working and living.

In my interviews with temps, time appears both to be an external force you cannot control and to offer a possibility to carve out a worklife and a lifestyle over which one is one's own time master, so to speak. Time is perceived both as a given, a taken-for-granted external factor to be reckoned with, and as a resource that one can use to tailor one's own worklife. 'Taking charge of one's own's work-life', as some informants phrased it, means confronting a diverse range of risks as well as possibilities. Security attained through stick-ing with conventional work routines is brittle, and will, at some point, crack. It betokens an inability to deal with the here and now, rather than providing a means for mastering it.

From the here-and-now orientation it follows that people will have to construct their own 'personalized, subjective temporalities' (Lash and Urry 1994: 245). The individual rendering of account will have to involve an amount of scenario-thinking to allow for various 'as-ifs' and improvizations. The career trajectory of a temp thus involves a complex spatial patterning together with a varied temporal rhythm. The imaginations of the temps need to be balanced against the canvas of moves that appear possible at a certain point in time. Marika, at Olsten in Stockholm, reflects on this theme:

> I really didn't think much about time before. I mean, I didn't really have to. But now that I'm temping I started to reflect on it. When I get a new assignment, I think: 'How long is this going to be? What kind of replacement are they looking for?' Because depending, I might wanna relate to them a little differently. And I also worry a little about the assignment after the next, and the next. And if I'm going to be able to have my summer holiday with my family. I mean, time has really become so much more prob-lematic! I just used not to pay much attention to it at all. And now I realize what a comfortable situation this was!

The reflexive relation to time in which temps engage involves to a large extent a balancing of external constraints and their own sub-jective preferences. Crucial for them, and for the upholding of a sense of continuity and meaningfulness of the work trajectories and identities, is the extent to which they can 'keep a particular narrative going' (Giddens 1991: 54). In a study of female temporary workers in New Zealand, Casey and Alach (2004) found that some women are striving to practise their own preferential employment arrangements in ways that actively challenge conventional economic assumptions of employment behaviour *and* traditional trajectories of women's lives. The continuous reflexivity with regards to time allows some temps to seek out their own tracks, while others are striving effortlessly to gain a sense of control over their narratives and trajectories.

This type of reflexivity may be seen as part of a broader 'culture of preparedness' (Jacobsson and Øygarden 1999), which aligns itself with the demands of labour markets in the new economy. To 'be prepared' also entails a particular kind of discipline. You should learn always to keep an evaluative eye on yourself, your routines and your capabilities. This preparedness, together with social versatility and scripting, makes up a distanciated form of employee control in mobile forms of work. Thus, whilst the mobility and transiency of flexible work may nurture notions of flexibility as a form of freedom to move at one's own will, what it entails is, rather, a form of scripted worklife, where the employee is fashioned into a particular type of accommodating and versatile employee identity (see Grey and Garsten 2001).

The temp is thus led to take on a reflexive stance towards time as well as space, and to constantly keep an eye on his or her relations to these aspects of work. The temp is led to understand that responsibility for continuous learning and upgrading of skills, for getting the next assignment and for being employable in the long run, is placed on herself, and that it has a great deal to do with being prepared for change. The technologies for putting this into practice show a striking degree of similarity across the temporary employee workforce, across corporations and across nations.

Conclusion: Learning the beat

The beat, or rhythm, of temping is different from that of much regular, long-term, administrative work. It is chunky, irregular and punctuated by *accelerandos*. The instantaneity and here-and-now orientation of flexible work colours much of the sociality of worklife and gives the culture of the industry a particular rhythm. The particular articulation of spatial and temporal patterns accounts for much of the experience of temping, as well as creating certain challenges in the management and control of flexible work.

In contemporary labour markets, temporality and mobility together make up an important stratifying dimension. In the previous chapter, we saw how patterns of mobility and the control of mobility work to provide a context for the work experience of temporary employees and how they structure work-related practices and perspectives. But equally important is the particular temporality that characterizes temporary agency work. The discontinuity in time, the short-term perspectives, the inability to plan and predict one's work trajectory, foster a certain readiness for change. Temps learn to orient themselves to the here and now, to the just-in-time logic of market demand. They do not fully control time, but are often controlled by it, their calendars decided largely by the agency and by the client. There is thus a sense in which temps are 'prisoners of the absolute' (cf. Lundmark 1993), of measured, precise and objective time, just like workers in mass-production plants, yet the time rhythms to which they learn to adapt are far more jerky and stochastic than that.

Temps are tied into circuits of mobility and temporal rhythms they learn to adapt to. Temping, as well as the management of temping, has been largely facilitated by the sense of time consciousness and time discipline that the majority of people bring to their jobs – a sense of punctuality, regularity and reliability, and an understanding of what constitutes a fair day's work (cf. Noon and Blyton 1997: 57). Even if the rhythm of temping differs from that of regular, full-time work, it thus relies on, and is influenced by, more generalized notions of time discipline and of the significance of time as a resource and control mechanism at work. In his classic work, *The Bureaucratic Phenomenon*, Michel Crozier described domination in all its varieties as linked up with closeness to the sources of uncertainty. His view still holds. Those who can keep their own actions unbound, unpredictable for others, who can decide on their own movements, while normatively regulating those of others, are the people who dominate. In Bauman's wordings, 'Domination consists in one's own capacity to escape, to disengage, to "be elsewhere", and the right to decide the speed with which all that is done – while simultaneously stripping the people on the dominated side of their ability to arrest or constrain their moves or slow them down.' For temps, there is the option of leaving the flexible labour market (which in some cases is not an easy choice), or of accepting the rules of the game while trying one's best to forge a degree of freedom.

Sennett, in sketching out the contours of what he calls the culture of the new capitalism, discusses the cultural consequences brought about by corporate downsizing, re-organizing and outsourcing. He posits three major challenges – time, talent and letting go of the past:

> Only a certain kind of human being can prosper in unstable, fragmentary social situations. This ideal man or woman has to address three challenges.
>
> The first concerns time: how to manage short-term relationships, and oneself, while migrating from task to task, job to job, place to place. If institutions no longer provide a long-term frame, the individual may have to improvise his or her life-narrative, or even do without any sustained sense of self (2006: 3–4).

With Sennett's words in mind, we will now look more closely at how Olsten go about searching for and fashioning this ideal man or woman.

5
Expectation and Evaluation

> Ask a temp, or anyone associated with the temporary worker industry, what the three most important qualities for successful temping are and that person will tell you flexibility, flexibility, flexibility.
>
> (Rogers 1996: 94)

Transformations in career and community can fruitfully be studied by addressing the practices that act upon people and their behaviour in specific domains of work, and the perspectives that underpin these practices. Attempts to reorganize and manage organizational and labour market change and to secure the engagement of people presuppose particular identities that are constructed at the juncture of organizational know-how and economical and political ideals (Foucault 1991, Miller and Rose 1995). For flexible organization to be realized, flexible workers have to be fashioned.

The work of temporary employees carries certain expectations as to what kind of assignments a temporary employee is supposed to take on, how these are to be carried out, and what is to be expected of the temporary employee in terms of skills, manners, attitude and appearance. Whilst temporary work is often described as offering both employees and clients a great deal of flexibility and variation, we see that it is also subject to standardization and regulatory constraints. Temporary employees are well aware that they are constantly being monitored and evaluated, and that this to a great extent is to do with the character of their employment; that it is temporary, mobile and dependent on their ability to satisfy the client as well as the employer. The evaluative gaze is a constant companion, and one that they learn to take for granted.

In this chapter, the expectations transmitted to temps and the practices of evaluation are highlighted. This involves looking at the normative demands put on them by temporary placement agencies and the clients, the kinds of characteristics stressed in advertisements, recruitment, assignments and evaluation, how they are put to work, and how the temporary employees themselves both perceive of and deal with them. The expectations placed on temporary employees influence how they conceive of their performance and their subjective identity. Flexible, temporary work thus entails subjecting oneself to a particular type of 'auditability', through continuous evaluations and check-ups from both agency and client organization. This evaluative gaze is a constant companion in the trajectory of a temp, and one that also engages the temp herself through techniques of 'responsibilization' and self-governance. We will look more closely at how temps are evaluated and rewarded as 'good' temps, and at some of the techniques by which certain understandings of flexibility are rendered powerful and authoritative while others are marginalized.[1]

Fostering flexibility

In temporary, flexible work, space and time are, as we have seen, rather discontinuous. This places a great deal of pressure on agencies and temps alike to learn the ropes quickly. The agency needs to be clear about expectations, competencies and job requirements. The temp has to find her feet rapidly in order to do the job successfully. Hence, temp agencies put a great deal of effort into making sure that temps are given the right kind of information and are socialized quickly into the world of temping. The care with which this is done is also indicative of the challenges of controlling, or managing, the temp while he or she is out on assignment. Since there is little, if any, possibility of overseeing work done in practice, the transmission of information, knowledge, advice and norms takes on a very explicit and often textualized character.

Rose, one of the assignment coordinators in California, who started her working life as a temp herself, stresses the fact that flexibility works both ways:

> From the outside, before you're really into temping, you associate flexibility with the temp's point of view and, to some extent, that's true. Temping can give you as much control over your life as you need. If you have the skills, if you are professional, and all that. But flexibility really works both ways. If you want to remain on our A list, you won't say no too often. You just don't.

Rose spells out clearly that it is the flexibility of the temp agency and the client that matters the most. My informants also reported that they rarely turn down or quit an assignment. Doing so would mean exposing yourself to the risk that the agency might not be too keen to engage you the next time. As Cindy, in Santa Clara, put it:

> I once wanted to refuse an assignment because I didn't really feel up to it, you know. I wasn't really interested in the job, which was a clerical one, rather uninteresting, and the company wasn't one of those hot ones, either. But I decided to go, because I don't really know what would have happened if I had turned it down. Maybe I'd be placed on the 'bad list' or in the archive, or something. ... Not that the agency tells you that you can, because they do let you know you can always say no, but I'm not sure.

Henson reports similar tales from his informants, saying that many suspect or quickly learn that refusing assignments should be done sparingly if at all, and that for fear of retribution in the form of down-time (i.e. unpaid time between assignments), temporaries often curtailed or minimized the use of their 'option' to refuse assignments (1996: 55–56).

Flexibility for the temporary employee has its limits and some accommodations have to be made. These are dependent on the needs of the agency and the client. To work as a temp and stay on the 'A list', you need to recognize this fact and be adaptable. It is the market for temporary services that provides the context of flexibility for the individual temporary employee.

We may stop briefly here to note that although the above citations are written with the US labour market in view, they are equally valid in Europe. The fact that many of the large staffing services, such as Olsten and Manpower, are US-based and operate through local agencies has contributed to the shaping of a transnational temping business with a clear American key signature. The idea of the self-reliant, competitive individual, taking on responsibility for his or her employability, is one that has gained a strong foothold in the European context, in which Sweden, despite its history of collective bargaining and organized interests, is no exception.

Screening for 'the Office Angel'

The procedures for screening and judging the applicant, for judging skills and competencies, as well as personal characteristics, may vary across sites, but they share some basic features. Everywhere, the needs of the client determine the matching. The deal is made by assignment coordinators, acting as matchmakers, connecting an available job applicant with a company looking for somebody to fill a vacancy. In this matching process, temp agencies find ways of appreciating just how well this particular candidate may be expected to perform the tasks, whether he or she may be expected to be punctual, to be flexible enough to bend to the needs of the client, whether he or she may represent the agency well – in short, to what extent the person may prove to be reliable and professional (see also Barley and Kunda 2004, Walter 2005).

Given the mobile and transient character of work, the matching process involves a degree of insecurity and risk as to how well the agency will be able to pick up on the needs of the client, how well the candidate will understand the requirements of the job, and how well he or she will 'fit' with the cultural and work style of the organization. Trust is thus an issue, and one that has to be developed and cultivated through the matching process (Henson 1996, Grey and Garsten 2001, Furusten and Garsten 2003, Walter 2005). The screening and matching thus goes on in an environment of uncertainty and risk, which boils down to the individual candidate as the focal point of judgement and evaluation.

A closer look at the process of getting a temporary job through a temporary employment agency reveals that there are standardized and highly routinized ways of recruiting an individual to a temporary assignment and of evaluating him or her, in Stockholm, as well in Santa Clara and Leeds. The streamlined and scripted procedures of getting a temp assignment are in stark contrast with the destandardization and flexibilization that is striven for in the set-up of employment contracts and in the rhetoric of desired employee characteristics. The competitive edge of flexibility does, however, gain a slightly more pronounced expression in the US and in the UK than in Sweden, where the rhetoric of competition is somewhat more subdued.

In Chapter 2, we gained an idea of what the screening procedure at Office Angels in Leeds looked like, as we accompanied Megan on her first visit to the agency office. At the Olsten Stockholm office, new applicants are also interviewed by an assignment coordinator upon appointment. In conjunction with the interview, she or he fills in a so-called 'Knowledge Form' ('Kunskapsblankett', my translation). This form asks for information on a number of topics, such as current employment and salary, educational and professional background, references, union membership, preferred working hours and region, any medical problems, as well as the kind of position applied for. Instead of having the applicant go through a test, as Megan did in Leeds, the Stockholm applicant is asked to rank his or her degree of proficiency in relevant areas on the form. Attached to the 'Knowledge Form' is a 'Development Card' ('Utvecklingskort', my translation), with five empty boxes for notes to be taken during future performance reviews ('utvecklingssamtal').

New Olsten recruits in Sweden are, like their American or British colleagues, also provided with brief, written information on the corporate structure and vision, with timesheets to fill in, as well as information on educational classes to be given in the near future. Introductory classes for new employees are given once a month, and as a new Olsten temp you are expected and encouraged to attend.

The first meeting with the agency, wherever it may be located, is crucial. The candidate needs to make a good impression as well as to establish a good personal connection with the assignment coordinator. An open and trusting relationship with the assignment coordinator is one of the major keys to the game. Many of my informants have stressed the significance of this relationship (we will see more of this in Chapter 6).

The screening process is only the beginning of a continuous series of normatively charged relations and evaluations. In the screening process, those who have not come across as versatile and pliant enough for temping are already excluded from the category of flexible workers. For those who remain, flexibility and evaluation are constant companions.

Flexibility: The double-edged sword

The value of 'being flexible' is often emphasized among temporary employees themselves. In interviews, it comes across as the most common response to questions about what it takes to be successful in the temp labour market. To be flexible, employees need to show a willingness to adapt to the expectations of the client regarding manners, task fulfilment, dress code and professionalism, as well as to the client's social environment. Being flexible means being able to bend, to adapt, to be elastic in relation to the client's needs and the agency's expectations.[2] In return, temping may offer the employee a relative degree of freedom: freedom to decide when and where to work, how many hours to put in, and in what kind of business to work. This is often referred to as the greatest advantage of temping.

For Lotta, 33 years old and working as a temp secretary with Olsten in Stockholm, the experience of flexibility is multifaceted. She likes her job with Olsten and finds it relatively easy to accommodate with the expectations of her clients:

> To me, flexibility is simply being able to do many things simultaneously. And being in control of things. I think that's mostly it. To have a lot of things going on and still be in control. That's flexibility. Flexibility is basically a good thing…in life in general. To be flexible and to foresee things and…. But then you can't always plan this job. Three people may suddenly appear through the door that we don't have any office space for. And we haven't received the information [from management about who the newcomers are, my insertion]. Then we have to know what to do with them. You can't plan everything, but then you can always ask. For example about this meeting or that. How many are coming? You have to be almost a detective. Check things up and…ask. Simply in order to create as few disturbances as possible.

Flexibility is, however, a double-edged sword. On the more negative side, it is often said to be the hardest part of the job, involving difficulties in defining the parameters of the task, maintaining a sense of integrity, and coping with being under constant scrutiny by the agency as well as the client. Birgitta, who is 27 years old and works for Olsten in Sweden as a financial assistant, reflects upon the different aspects of flexibility in this way:

> You absolutely have to be flexible all the time... I define flexibility as being able to re-prioritize your tasks. You have to check continuously to see if something more important comes up. The most ideal situation is to work on one task at a time, finish it, and then proceed to the next. That way you are in control. But... that does not work here. If the sales manager says, 'Shit! In ten minutes I have a very important meeting with a customer. Could you please help me with the contract?' then you have to shift immediately... and be service-minded. I can't find a better word for it. You have to like it, to give it your best. And take on tasks that aren't really yours. But it's also important that you don't abandon yourself to them. You actually have to say no if they ask you... to polish their shoes. It may be very hard, since it's not in the papers what's part of your tasks. The boundary is unclear. So it's up to your own judgement. ... When you start to know people, then you may start to say no. 'Cause you do get used. You do. 'Cause they know... you are in a very delicate position. If you do it wrong you may have to go. And in such a position, it's clear that I give more than I would otherwise have done. I would have been a lot more cocky on my former job than I am here. ... And you know it's a very important client for Olsten. So pride can be tough, sometimes.

For Birgitta, defining the limits of flexibility is difficult. Being flexible, switching tasks and being service-minded, is important to her chances of staying on the books. It is a way of being employable. To her, it relates to integrity and pride, which may be hard to uphold in the face of client expectations and of loyalty to the temp agency.

That temps are talked about, and talk about themselves, as 'flexible' has an impact on how they come to understand themselves and how they come to act. Labelling is part and parcel of the process by which people are constituted as particular kinds of employees in organizational contexts. It is a way of 'making up people', as Hacking (1986) describes it. As the label of 'flexible employee' is placed onto the temps, they learn to think about themselves with a particular inventory of ideals at hand, and are, to some extent, transformed in the process (see also Garsten 2004).

The right attitude

As we saw earlier (in Chapter 3), being a flexible temp also means being someone who can be relied on to be sent anywhere, to whatever client needs his or her services, and who can adapt to different tasks. A 'good temp' is also someone who can adopt a friendly attitude and avoid getting involved in company gossip or conflicts. At an early stage, temps are also made to reflect more consciously on the kind of impression they are making on the client, and on how to manage and improve this. Increased attention to one's attitude and manners is a significant aspect of the construction and maintenance of the temp identity.

Emotions, as constructed in social interactions, and as outcomes of the ways in which systems of meaning are made and negotiated between people, are an integral part of organizational life. In the organizational setting, managing emotion becomes a part of creating a sense of commitment and belonging, as well as of controlling the actions and attitudes of members of the organization. 'Feeling rules' give social pattern to acts of emotions management. 'Feeling rules are standards used in emotional conversation to determine what is rightly owed and owing in the currency of feeling. Through them, we tell what is "due" in each relation, each role' (Hochshild 1983: 18). Our sensations, thoughts and feelings are labelled and displayed in accordance with the social and cultural context that defines and provides the rules. So also at Olsten, where the service-oriented and client-based character of work requires that the temp is highly attentive and alert to the feeling rules of the temp agency and not least that of the client organization.

To manage emotions also becomes part of the job, so to speak. Having to present the right – or prescribed – emotional appearance to the client involves real emotional labour on the part of the temp. Olsten tries to ensure that temps are aware of this, and comply as far as possible; they do so by carefully screening for the 'right' candidate, by inculcating scripts and carrying out regular evaluation procedures.

The need for 'emotional labour' – that is, the management of feeling to create a publicly observable facial and bodily display (Hochschild 1983) – relates strongly to the intermediary role that temps perform between client and temp agency. As Jacky Krasas Rogers (1995: 152) points out: 'The agency relationship creates a stronger need for emotional labor in two ways. First, the temporary worker actually has two jobs: one as a clerical worker at the hiring company and another as a representative of the temporary employment agency.' Even though her material builds on interviews with temporaries in the US, the basic condition of the agency relationship is valid in the UK and Sweden as well. Like the temps interviewed by Rogers in southern California, the temps at Olsten are highly aware that they are representatives of the temporary employment agency, 'ambassadors' as some informants put it, and that future assignments may depend on their ability to accommodate to the clients.

Temporaries, then, learn that they must avoid expressing their personal views or emotions too much, and that to be successful at work they must engage in 'emotional labour' to disguise or manage their personal attitudes and feelings. As Hochschild (1983: 7) says, 'This labor requires one to induce or suppress feeling in order to sustain the outward countenance that produces the proper state of mind in others.' Engaging in emotional labour is understood to be more than situational adjustment; it is a skill acquired through having done temping for a while, learning how to be socially flexible and to have the 'right attitude'. Henson (1996: 124) argues: 'Looking submissive or adopting a suitable demeanour with the appropriate mix of cooperation, deference, and cheer was essential for the successful performance of the temporary role and was expected and demanded by temporary agencies.'

Whilst I did not experience that submissiveness was in any way encouraged or embraced, showing a friendly face and being alert to client needs were important.

The discipline and control that come with the highly mobile and temporally fragmented work of temping require a particular form of social versatility. The general expectation of a temp is that of being pleasant, attentive, courteous – and even well groomed – so as to fit in with the client work environment. This social versatility is necessary for the smooth completion of the job. To upset expectations, to behave rudely, to question or argue with the client's requirements, to fail to connect socially in a smooth and non-committing way, or to dress inappropriately, are among the definite 'no-no's' of temping.

For one, temps are advised to avoid behaviour or topics of conversation that may lead to conflict. Temps are told that they must not to burden the client with their views on the company's routines ... and what they think of its managers' (in 'To remember while working with Olsten' – 'Att tänka på när jag arbetar i Olsten', my translation). The leaflet 'An introduction to temping with Office Angels' provides similar advice and a checklist of appropriate behaviour. Here, one reads: 'Tell US if you have a complaint not someone else working in the company.' Valerie, who works for Office Angels in Leeds, pays careful attention to these rules. When we met she was on maternity leave. We sat in the living room of her house on the outskirts of Leeds, while her baby girl was sleeping in the bedroom. Being on leave, she had had plenty of time to reflect on what temping amounts to:

> The hardest thing is when you walk into politics. You, know, any company has lots of politics and as a temp you don't understand who's who. So, you have to be very careful – not getting, you know, involved in any of that – and to be very, very professional. I think that's what's nice about temping. If you get good temps in the company, they keep the company sane. Because ... no one there is perm, [stays] long enough to cause much trouble, you know.

Part of learning the 'feeling rules' of temping is also about learning when to display a 'bounded emotionality' (cf. Martin et al. 2000). A more impersonal approach, a slightly more suppressed emotional display, can sometimes prevent the temp from becoming too involved in the emotional culture of the client organization. Learning when and how to 'stay out of' emotionally charged situations and to display a more 'professional', aloof or neutral attitude is also part of the job.

The gracious manners of temps may seem innocent strategies for getting along in a competitive labour market. While they assist in smoothing relations and facilitating new deals, they also work to control temps in ways that contribute both to a feminized form of service work and to the gendering of work practices and organizations. Hall, in an article entitled 'Smiling, deferring, and flirting: Doing gender by giving good service' (1993), argues that personnel practices, divisions of labour, and the normative expectations placed on employees tend to systematically differentiate between male and female employees, thereby creating a 'gendered work organization'. This is also valid for the administrative temping business in general, characterized by a service-oriented approach, including a strong emphasis on manners and making a good impression.

Dressed for success

Temporaries are also advised and taught how to dress to look professional and fit in with the client's work environment. Dress code is not unimportant. A good temp, like most white- or pink-collar workers, must know how to dress appropriately. Sometimes, appearance even overshadows ability and skill in securing assignments. This may happen when the job is a representative one, such as in a reception, and where the external signs of professionalism are important. More often, though, dress code is particularly important during the initial meeting with the client, when first impressions are made, after which the temp can afford gradually to pay less attention to her outfit.

As in Leeds and Santa Clara, temps at Olsten in Stockholm are given written as well as oral guidelines as to how to dress:

> When you are on an assignment you are Olsten's public face. Therefore it is important that you dress professionally and that you use Olsten's PIN [i.e. needle]. Dress up a little for your first day on the assignment. We use neither jeans nor leggings at Olsten. ('A job to love' – 'Ett jobb att älska', my translation)

At one temp agency I visited in the Silicon Valley, the new recruits were even showed a 15-minute film on appropriate professional attire. The agency emphasized that temporary employees should carefully observe and conform with the client company's standards, as well as those of the temp agency. Temps were advised to 'take their cue' from others at the workplace and make sure not to dress too casually on the first day of their new assignment. I was given the opportunity to see this film myself as part of the interview with one of the managers. I recall that detailed instructions were given on the appropriate length of skirt, height of heels, neckline, size of earrings, and much else besides. Also, examples were given as what not to wear: very short skirts, jeans, sandals, long earrings, red lipstick, and so on. (This is when I realized that I would probably have been a failure as a temp candidate, not wearing tights with my skirt, and wearing comfortable sandals.) A professional appearance not only demands that you 'dress corporate', but this style itself implies notions of what is gender-appropriate and 'feminine' (see also Henson 1996: 115–124, for similar findings). And choosing the proper outfit is, through these textualized and mediatized guidelines, part of the script that the temp has to learn.

Olsten temps are sometimes provided with a business suit to facilitate dressing appropriately for a new assignment. While the suit sometimes comes in handy since the temps do not have to think about what to wear for a new assignment, few of my informants reported wearing it regularly. It does, however, provide them with a degree of comfort to know that it is there, should they need it. One temp told me she always had hers ready on a coat hanger at her client's office. Birgitta, who works for the Stockholm office, expressed some irritation about the anxieties of dressing correctly:

> Tiresome matter, I must say, [dressing]. Because you are poorly paid in this business. Well, I myself am well paid, but there are many girls who earn very little. And you have huge demands on you at the client's. It's OK here, we are rather sloppy here. It's great [*laughing*] .... But I was on four, five assignments before this one and on two of them they were really strict... snobbish, sort of. So it's like they check out what brands you wear. How are you supposed to meet those demands? It's impossible! To me, it was really hard to feel that... you are examined.... Olsten lends you a suit. Thank heavens! I liked that, to have it just in case. A navy blue suit you might not feel like buying yourself. That's not everybody's style. And it costs a great deal. But it's a great idea.

Olsten temps are generally well dressed and well mannered, with a ready smile on their lips. I was told that you needed to be 'well groomed', to pay attention to your haircut, your nails, and your skin to make a really good impression. Clothing and make-up can turn into a costly part of worklife. Many of my informants emphasized that what to wear at work is a matter of some importance and part of a good performance. Generally, they said, it is better to dress professionally on the first day. Then you can take your cue from other people in the office, and adapt your dress accordingly (see also Garsten and Turtinen 2000: 188–191). I was often told that getting the proper outfit ready was part of the routine of moving to a new assignment in a new workplace. The night before being on call, or when about to start a new assignment, temps would make sure their clothes were clean, ironed and laid out ready for them to get dressed quickly. Such scripting routines would save them some of the troubles of choosing what to wear and what style to conform to: 'corporate', 'casual', smart' or some other style (see also Chapter 3).

Lisa, who works for Olsten to finance her studies for a doctorate in archaeology, thinks that the weight placed on dress code, and that the way it enters into the evaluation of your performance, is one of the more stressful aspects of temping:

> I think it's hard, feeling that you are constantly being scrutinized. And after all, it's more relaxing to wear a sweater under your jacket, like you and I are, rather than that formal blouse every day. And high heels. And if you are with the same client for two weeks what happens is that they keep an eye on your clothes, make sure you don't wear the same outfit every day. ... You need to look clean, well-dressed and proper.

The exposed situation that temps often experience can be aggravated during pregnancy.

Fran, who is now on maternity leave from Olsten in Santa Clara, tells me about the insecurity she felt about dress code when she was pregnant:

> *Fran*: The first day is always the hardest. The first day is hard because you have to overcome the fact that you are pregnant. You have to overcome that fact! You have to get there and find the place. And I didn't really want to spend a lot of money on

clothing. And I think, when you are temping, if you want to be good at it, you have to dress smartly. No matter what the position. Especially the first day, because you don't know what the company is like. And sometimes they'd specify a dress code, but I always think it's best to be cautious and dress more smartly than casual.

Christina: So how would you usually dress?

Fran: Well, it was summertime so I would usually be wearing a dress. The first day it may even have been trousers and a shirt. But usually something coloured, you know. Something that maybe looked like it was smart. And then depending on how it went and what kind of company it was. And of course in the Valley they're very casual. So I could wear flowery dresses and more comfortable clothing. But usually I still wore stricter outfits. Smart shoes and stockings and a dress. I never went for tights and a T-shirt, for example. That wasn't something I would do.

In Fran's case, being pregnant enhanced the caution she would normally feel about dress code. She was nervous about not being 'taken seriously' as a young pregnant woman, and as a temp. She told me how being pregnant puts you in a particularly vulnerable situation in the labour market. This is also one reason she chose to work as a temp, because she felt that this was not the perfect time to start her career. She wanted the flexibility in relating to work pragmatically that comes with temping. But being pregnant made her feel even more vulnerable.

There are of course some situations where dress code is not that important, or at least not given that much attention. Susan, working from the Santa Clara office, talked about an assignment she was on when dress code did not matter that much:

I think it depends on where you're working. When I was over at that company it didn't really matter much what we wore. Nobody really cared…. In fact, I was on another assignment they sent me on where they really couldn't have cared less. In fact my boss told me. He says. 'Oh,' he says, 'you don't' even need to dress up'. He says, 'You wear Levi's in here'. You know…. But always on your first day you dress up. Until you find out, you know, what people are wearing.

Learning to be flexible is to a large extent the acquisition of a specific sort of female reflexivity. It involves being attentive to the needs of the client, in terms of what tasks are to be performed, but also paying attention to appropriate dress code, manners and the like – making sure they are not only professional but also gender-appropriate. The gendering of flexibility reveals itself in the subtle forms through which a feminine code of conduct is fostered: one that is marked by social versatility, sensitivity and responsiveness to others' expectations and needs.[3] The emphasis on dress code and manners is, in fact, an additional job requirement which, while positively striking to every onlooker, becomes invisible as a form of labour (cf. Freeman 2001: 215). Flexible work, then, embraces attitudes, behaviours, expectations, as well as dress code. It involves a self-disciplining and self-governance of the body and the emotions, a constant watching over oneself, as well the acceptance of being watched. The individual here becomes something of a relay of evaluative practices in which they are both subjected to the evaluation of others, and encouraged to engage in self-evaluation.

The preoccupation with dress code also underlines the fact that dressing up the temps involves a particular modality of power that works at the very juncture between the freedom to express one's uniqueness and self-understanding through dress and the imposition of globalizing, corporate standardization. The enhanced preoccupation with outward appearance that is generally so visible in globalized corporations has steadily made its way into the temping industry. And since this modality of power works through the personal attire of the temps, close to the body, it becomes all the more powerful. With Keenan (2001: 186), we note that dress codes, and the control of them, are in no way innocent organizational forms of control:

> Whenever dress codes are imposed for whatever reason – health and safety, esprit de corps, corporate identity, a sense of equity, group discipline, collective order, human resources management and personnel control, the fancies of employers and owners, *force majeur*, loyalty to tradition, and so forth – those who would remain vigilant about the small, basic, perennially vulnerable freedoms that matter in everyday life, should be on guard with a healthy hermeneutic of suspicion.

Audited temps: The evaluative gaze

In so far as flexibility is a normative tool, it is also put to work in the context of evaluation of performance. The rise of what has been called the 'audit culture' and the associated techniques of accountability are clearly evinced in the temporary staffing business. Seemingly mundane and routine practices of evaluation may have profound effects on the future assignments, salary levels and career development of temps. Such practices may be understood as 'audit technologies' that function as instruments for new forms of governance and power. They embody a new rationality and morality designed to engender amongst the temps particular norms of conduct and professional behaviour. They are agents for the creation of new kinds of subjectivity: 'self-managing individuals who render themselves auditable' (Shore and Wright 2000: 57). As Shore and Wright (2000: 58) have noted, ideas and practices of auditing are but one expression of a global process of neoliberal economic and political transformation that have migrated across sectors and across national boundaries, and taken on particular local forms in specific local contexts. For the temporary staffing sector, the practices of evaluation can in large part be traced back to the management strategies of their American headquarters.

As we have seen in Chapters 3 and 4, temping is characterized by a 'manufactured uncertainty' (Giddens 1994: 184) in both spatial and temporal terms. Many aspects of working life, such as if and when there will be a next assignment and where one will go for the next one, are undecided until shortly before the current assignment is terminated. The continuity of work is organized only in terms of 'scenario thinking', in the way of an as-if construction of possible future outcomes. And since transience has become a more or less permanent condition, the temps have no choice but to reflect critically upon their own, individual role in influencing future work trajectories.

Olsten emphasizes the importance of continuous learning in order to stay 'on the books' and to be 'employable'. In the folder 'A job to love', Olsten stresses the importance of ' continuous development':

> We know that it is important to develop one's competence within one's professional area. We can offer you that. We can also offer

you more. During 1997 we are enlarging our learning departments, making them into modern, comfortable and easily accessible knowledge centres. These are open to you, as much as you want. Come on in during the day or in the evening, practise on a switchboard or surf the Internet. Test your knowledge of Excel or learn PowerPoint from the basics, everything is possible! The knowledge and competence you have when you start working with us, we'd like you to maintain and develop. The centres are at the disposition of both you and our customers. Your chances of varied assignments increase with the breadth of your competence. Take advantage of the chance you get through Olsten to learn something new.

To be truly flexible requires much more than adaptation. What is needed is an ability to learn, to communicate, to cooperate, to judge one's own situation, to make diagnoses, to understand and embrace change, as well as mobility. This also requires continuous learning and upgrading of skills. Most of this is done by the temp him- or herself outside office hours and is unpaid. The agency provides the computers and software they consider appropriate as well as testing routines that may help temps qualify for higher pay. But it is the responsibility of the individual to create the time to actually practise and learn, something many of them find difficult to do after a full day's work.

Temps at Olsten are always evaluated after a completed assignment. The practices of evaluation are intended to make temps aware of the necessity of continuous training, development and improvement. For the agency, it is part of the fostering of a continuous and market-driven kind of reflexivity. It is also a way of keeping track of the performance of their dispersed workforce.

The manner in which the evaluation takes place is highly standardized. While the testing that a new candidate has to go through before getting an assignment concentrates on the skills of the candidate, the evaluation concentrates on the perceived traits of character and behaviour of the temp. In Stockholm, an 'Evaluation Form' ('Utvärderingsblankett', my translation) is used, on which details of the performance, including punctuality, attitude and skill level are rated. Furthermore, the individual temp goes through a performance review once a year. During the review, the temp may also share his or her experiences of temping: which assignments have been most or least appreciated, and why. However, the temp does not make an evaluation of his or her experiences with clients in any routinized way. Depending on the character of the temporary employee–assignment coordinator relationship, the temp may informally make some sort of an evaluation, but this is not archived or kept as a record, as are client evaluations of temps. Client evaluations are considered to be very valuable to the agency, and as they are received they are attached to the bundle of papers that together make up the record of the individual temp.

At the Office Angels agency in Leeds, the evaluation form that the client fills in at the end of an assignment is headed 'Assessment'. On the assessment form, the client types in the name and capacity of assignment of the temp and the respondent's name, title and company. The following aspects are then evaluated:

- Enthusiasm
- Understanding of instruction
- Skill level
- Accuracy
- Punctuality
- Appearance
- Overall suitability

The client is asked to rate the above criteria as 'Excellent', 'Good', Adequate' or Poor'. The following question is then posed: Would you specifically request this person to work for you again, if the need arises?'

On the form, there is also a statement as to the value of this assessment:

OFFICE ANGELS temporaries are rated and rewarded through constant appraisal of task achievement and attitude to work.

Your own assessment and comments would be extremely useful in this process and we would be grateful for your input. An addressed envelope is attached for your reply.

Similar forms are also sent to clients in Santa Clara and Stockholm.

As we can see, what is evaluated is not just skills and suitability for the task, but a whole range of aspects that have to do with the personal characteristics of the temp, with attitude and service-orientation. Flexibility thus turns into a regulatory force through processes and techniques by which aspects of work that are not limited to task performance but engage with the subjectivity of the person are embraced and made auditable.

Temps are generally aware of the fact that they are being evaluated, and consider it 'good' and 'reasonable'. There is a general understanding about the competitive character of the labour market, and the normality of being evaluated. They tend to say that a good evaluation helps them in getting a good assignment. Mary, who is 25 years old and has been working with Olsten for three years, expresses well a common view among temps:

> *Mary*: We have, like, little performance reviews or whatever you call them with our contact persons at Olsten, and then we talk. At that time, they have had this evaluation with the client so they will know what the client says, and then they talk to us, and we will know what the client thinks about us. We get to know what they have said about us. ... And then we may reply to that.... We may not write anything, but we do have these talks with our contact persons so that's good.
>
> *Christina*: Do you think this works well or are you nervous about being evaluated?
>
> *Mary*: No, don't think I am [nervous]. I mean, I can only do my best. ... There has not been any problem yet, so no, I haven't [been nervous], 'cause then it wouldn't work. ... You can't work well with everyone. You don't fit in with every company. ... You can only do your best. If they want something different you can't really do anything about it. Or, you can always improve, but, well, that's the way it is. So it's not something I go around thinking about, that it could be unpleasant or something like that.

Like Mary, most temps interviewed regard the evaluation as a normality, something they would not think could be questioned. Rather, they subject themselves quite unproblematically to the routines of the temp agency. And if reflecting on them, they tend to accept the necessity of evaluations. How would it work otherwise? It would seem here that the 'normalizing gaze' has conferred upon evaluations a taken-for-granted status. Not only have they been made into routines the temps comply with, but into routines they tend to take for granted, contribute to, and even welcome. What would the alternatives be?

Temps learn to take it upon themselves to become 'responsibilized' (Grey 1997), to perform in accordance with the demands of the client and the agency and to collaborate in making visible those aspects of their performance, appearance, manners and skills that are to be evaluated by the client and the agency after the assignment. This responsibilization involves agreeing to the evaluative procedures as well as a continuous self-monitoring.

Flexibility is fostered further by incentives. To enhance and reward professional competence and appropriate behaviour, the temp agencies regularly announce awards that are made public among the temps and staff. Olsten in Sweden confers recognition through the award of a 'Golden Ant' on a yearly basis to temps in different categories. There are, for example, the categories of the 'Receptionist of the Year', the 'Accountant of the Year', the 'Olsten Employee of the Year', and the 'Newcomer of the Year'. The winners are made public in the newsletter *Bullen*, and rewarded with a diploma and an oversized gold-coloured ant which are presented to them at the yearly customer-and-employee party. These awards work to encourage identification with agency expectations and to foster acceptance of the company's claims on their performance.

Shortly before my interview with Lotta, she had been awarded the Golden Ant for her outstanding contributions, together with a colleague of hers. As she told me about it, she glowed with excitement and delight at the attention and affirmation she had been given:

> It's so much fun when they're about to nominate. ... We were all sitting at a table in the Concert Hall when they [one of the managers at Olsten, my remark] announced the name of my colleague. And we looked at each other, she and I, and then they read my name. But that's me! [*laughing*]. You get completely ... . Then one doesn't hear a word. You float into some sort of [*laughing*] dream world. ... We got a diploma, with an ant. And then we received a large golden ant made of cellophane paper or something that we could place in the Concert Hall. It was such a lot of fun [*laughing*] ... 'Cause

then you get official recognition. That's really great. And then everybody is sitting there watching and you walk up to the stage and…. You get really nervous. It really is fun. And it's so much fun because so many of my colleagues have also received these awards.

Awards, like the public announcement of the Golden Ant, gives visibility to the good and desired performance of temporary workers. Individuals become conscious of themselves as 'performers', seemingly 'in control' of their performance (cf. Munro 1999). On occasions like this, what constitutes good performance and a good temp is made explicit and visible. The codified expectations of pamphlets and introductory courses are given content and concrete expression, and the individual temp stands out as the performing agent.

Conclusion: The velvet glove of control

Under flexible forms of work, soft means of power are refined into ever more subtle techniques using technologies and routines of evaluation to make the temps accountable and transparent. They are taught to conceive of themselves in particular terms: 'We are members of an organization who provides flexible services to our client organizations. My job is to represent the agency in the best way I can.' The velvet glove of control works by sensitizing the temps to their own responsibility for development and evaluation of skills and attitudes.

The self-evaluative gaze is learnt by temps as part of the job, so to speak. It is a way of adapting to existing structures and normative demands, which is built up alongside the rhetoric of the flexible labour market as freedom from traditional and hindering structures and increased opportunities of constructing one's own life-narrative and work-biography. Lash (1994: 120) emphasizes the need to address what he refers to as 'the structural conditions of reflexivity'. What underpins the reflexivity of temps is a web of global networks of corporate structures, in which the conditions for temporary work are to a large extent determined by the place of temps in these structures.

Through the evaluation procedures, the temps are rendered transparent for the agency, and to some extent also for the client organization, while the temp agency and the client organization remain largely opaque for the temps. The evaluative gaze is uni-directional, and does not provide for an alternative rendering of results. Deviations from what is considered normal – being flexible, reliable, ready to move, dressing appropriately and showing the right attitude – are made visible and consequential. The temp has to agree to be evaluated, and made transparent, for him or her to move along in the flexible labour market.

This kind of soft power, or 'concertive control' (Barker 1999) appears to work best in post-bureaucratic organizations, where decen-tralized, participative designs are adopted, and in which control by formal rules and hierarchy have been abandoned in favour of consensual and values-based actions (Kärreman and Alvesson 2001, Clegg et al. 2005: 172, 183). In such organizations, employees learn to collaborate to develop the means of their own control. This is what we see happening in dispersed organizations like Olsten, where temps are drawn into practices and ideologies of evaluation, learn to accept the evaluative gaze, and eventually become their own gover-nors. This is a form of power that presupposes the 'agency' of individuals (Meyer and Jepperson 2000). It is also a highly seductive form of power, which works by invoking freedom, individuality, responsibility and development, and which is dressed up as benevolent and empowering (Foucault 1991).

6
Contingent Communities

Place: Santa Clara, coffee shop on El Camino Real
Time: Tuesday Lunchtime, February, 1999
Topic of conversation: Social relations at Olsten
Nathalie: One thing I have found is that temping can be quite
lonely. At the same time as you are there, doing a job, you are
not involved. It's a two-edged sword. You can just get on with
what you are doing and leave at the end of the day. You don't
bring work home with you. You don't build relationships.
People don't. They're not interested in spending time with you
socially. Because there's no need to. And it's pointless. 'Cause
you're leaving in a month.

Whatever happened to workplace community?

The concept of community usually brings to mind 'rather more
tangible, small, face-to-face entities, unproblematically situated in
space', as Hannerz phrases it (1995: 92). As for work communities, we
have tended to associate them with – spatially – relatively bounded
groups of people and ideas, connected to each other through interdependencies of various kinds. But with connections, relations and
interdependencies now being redistributed in space and time, what
happens to workplace communities?

There are a number of more or less apocalyptic versions of the loss
of meaning at work, or the sense of community, and of identity.
Many writers have signalled the decline of work as a shaper of
community and identity (for example, Rifkin 1995). Temporary

agency work does call established ways relating to colleagues and employers into question. The mobile, transient and competitive character of work means that relations with colleagues are often of a fragmented and episodic character. It is, in fact, rather unlikely that temps will put down deep roots in any of the places they work in, or develop strong attachments to other temporaries or the staff at the temporary staffing agency. Expectations that long-term relations will unfold out of continuous involvement with others in an individual employment setting are no longer there. Prepared for change and upheaval, temporary agency workers expect their stay to be more or less temporary, and hence, they expect little in the sense of continuity and community to arise out of their involvements with workmates, either at the client's, or at the temporary employment agency. I agree with Bauman (1995, 1998a,b) that the discontinuities of space and time mean that work communities also risk becoming more contingent.

On the other hand, the global interconnectedness of organizations, the pervasiveness of media technology and the de-territorialization of organizational structures mean that the work community may now be constructed beyond local organizational contexts (Hannerz 1995: 91–101). Members of organizations now have at their disposal a wide variety of 'infrastructural technologies' in Calhoun's terms (1992) through which they can maintain close contact with dispersed colleagues. Such infrastructural technologies provide a means for organizations to create postulated, 'imagined communities' of global reach (Anderson 1983). There is thus a sense in which communities may well become more densely connected through mediated communication. In a sense, then, it is not so much a matter of 'stronger' or 'weaker' communities and identities, but of transforming contexts for the formation of community and identity; of changing practices of acting upon these, and changing notions of attachment and belonging. The globalization of labour markets and work practices is changing our notions of 'community', and so also for temps (cf. Albrow et al. 1997).

Work, even in the temping business, continues to be a key site for the formation of persons, of communities and of meaning. With Miller and Rose (1995: 428), I believe we need to look more closely at the practices that act upon human beings and human conduct in specific domains and the kinds of systems that underpin these to understand how identity and community become contested and transformed. Work is a central social activity and one that connects the individual with larger social, cultural and economic structures.[1] In and through work, we discover who we are, what our priorities are, and we discover the multiplicity of ways in which we can relate to others. I thus agree with Barley and Kunda (2001) in saying that in order to understand post-bureaucratic forms of organizing, as well as the subject positions that are created by and for individuals, we need to 'bring work back in'.

The transorganizational patterns of movement can thus enable the mobilization of community among dispersed groups of temps, as well as causing their fragmentation. The discontinuous nature of temporary work means that a sense of community at work has to be built up from premises that are strikingly different from those experienced under long-term, regular employment at a particular workplace. The challenges of establishing such relations and the resulting nature of community and collegial relations are discussed in this chapter.

Temps and regulars: Close-up strangers

In the workplace, temps are sometimes easily distinguished from regulars. For a start, they often occupy particular kinds of positions in the client organization, their contract with the client is temporary, they may wear badges of a different colour, and they are not automatically invited to social events at the client organization. Inside an organization, it is often clear who is a temp and who is a regular. At one of the larger American IT companies in Sweden, for example, temps wear red badges saying 'non-HP' (not a regular employee of Hewlett Packard), they are not included in all email address lists, and they may not be included in all the company meetings. Their email addresses also have 'non-HP' as part of the identification.

Managers of client organizations often strategically build these categories into their organizations and lock them into place. Particular services are designed for outsourcing, particular functions are externalized, and extra manpower is leased as needed. Kalleberg and Marsden (2005) describe how what they call 'external workers' tend to supplement regular workers engaged in more central activities and exclusively perform more peripheral ones; employers are also more apt to supervise 'external workers'. As we have seen earlier (in Chapter 3) 'good' client organizations to work for are those that have developed a readiness for receiving temps inside their organizational boundaries; that have developed the routines and scripting of relations needed for flexibility to operate. Hence, flexibilization also involves a great deal of standardization in the making of organizational positions and identities.

From the point of view of the client organization, then, a temp is usually an outsider, a stranger, importing new qualities into the group. Whilst the temp may be very welcome and integrate easily into the work group, his or her workmates at some point or other start to ask themselves how long the temp is expected to be with them, to what extent he or she can be expected to understand the particularities of their workplace and the people working there, and to what extent she can be relied upon as a trustworthy colleague. Having a temp in the organization for a longer period of time often means that the regulars of the organization start to reflect on and discuss the boundaries of the organization among themselves. Particularly so if the temp is well integrated into the work environment and her status as an outsider to the organization tends to be blurred.

From this point of view, we may thus view temps and regulars as representing two distinct social categories in the workplace.

However, categories are not specific sets of people or fixed attributes, but standardized, movable social relations, as Tilly has it (1995: 66). They need not rely on objectively verifiable characteristics. The temp's and the regular's identity may be culturally afloat. It may in fact be quite difficult to figure out who is a regular and who is not. For one, client organizations vary in their integration of temps. Some readily invite temps to feel part of the community at the workplace, by inviting them to parties, sharing access to facilities such as fitness centres, and not minding too much about who is an insider and who is an outsider. Temps may thus not be clearly identifiable as a distinct social category. As I was interviewing at Apple Computer in Silicon Valley, it happened a number of times that I discovered that the employee I was interviewing was not in fact an Apple employee, but a temp, formally 'non-Apple'. The managers and employees at Apple did not normally pay a great a deal of attention to this difference in status, except in relation to product development and other sensitive activities (see Garsten 1994). Many of these temps were, in Pink's terminology, 'permatemps' (2001: 219), individuals who work full-time for a company, sometimes for years, doing the same job as regular employees – but who are hired through a temp agency so that responsibility for the provision of benefits does not fall upon the company, but upon the temp agency. Long-term temps melt into the social milieu of the client organization in a way that makes everyday distinctions insignificant. This is confirmed by informants at another large IT company, who say long-term temps are often treated as regulars, until suddenly the distinction is highlighted when sensitive corporate information is to be shared, strategic decisions are to be taken, or the like.

Nevertheless, temps and regulars may be seen to constitute 'paired categories', with actors on both sides engaged in mutual labelling. As Tilly points out, categorical work always involves imputing distinctive qualities to actors on either side of boundaries (1995: 67).

The most common situation is, after all, that temps and regulars are relatively sure about who is who and what kinds of qualities may be associated with either side. In the view of regulars, temps do not show the same loyalty to the company on whose premises they work as they themselves do; they are not committed to the company to the same extent; they do not assume the same degree of responsibility for the job; nor are they as involved with local co-workers as the regulars themselves.

From the perspective of temps, regulars may be less committed to the task assigned to them, since their continued employment is not dependent on their getting the job done as quickly and professionally as possible in the way that it is for temps. They tend to take their position for granted in a way that temps do not. Regulars may be polite and welcoming, but they are often more self-assured than temps and tend sometimes to treat temps in a somewhat bullying manner.

If reinforced by financial restraints, reorganizations or corporate events surrounded by secrecy, the perceived difference in categorical identity may become more clearly salient. Here, the distinction and the boundary between temps and regulars becomes a socially or politically charged boundary. Representing oneself as a regular or a temp then establishes distance. In such cases, regulars and temps may engage in 'authenticating performances' (cf. Tilly 1995: 219) that establish unity, worthiness, loyalty and commitment – for example by showing off badges, using local slang expressions unintelligible to others, and in other ways displaying difference and exclusion. I was told of this happening at a client's in the electronics business in Stockholm, where the company was under heavy strain from re-organizations and lay-offs. One of the temps, Lukas, told me the regulars were not very happy with his presence, and tried their best to shut him out, by engaging in conversations about people and events he could not tap into, or by talking their own 'corporate mumbo-jumbo' replete with technical abbreviations.

It is important to point out that the categories of temp and regular do not pervade working life so thoroughly as to rule out crosscutting categorical memberships (see Tilly 1995: 67). In Sweden, temps are often regular employees of the staffing services and enjoy the benefits of regular membership there. This means that temps are *both* regulars and temps, depending on one's perspective. They represent at least two categories at the same time, that of temp being the more visible one on the premises of the client organization. Regular contact with the employing staffing services via telephone, email or on-site visits by assignment coordinators work to reassure temps and make visible the significance of their simultaneously being regulars. Temps learn to do the work of two categories simultaneously and to draw on their different repertoires.

The categorical distinction between temps and regulars also shows some local variation. The Silicon Valley area is one in which temps have worked alongside regulars for a relatively long time, and where large segments of the labour market are dependent on large numbers of temps. The distinction between temps and regulars is thus not as visible as it is in Sweden, where the norm of regular employment contracts still lingers on more strongly in the labour market. Even so, the distinction is evident in larger, global ways of organizing work, and in categorical sets that already operate visibly elsewhere.

Market logics: Substitutability and competitiveness

One of the more intriguing aspects of temping is that it involves a simultaneous notion of uniqueness and substitutability. In many ways, temping requires a flexible adaptation to the unique demands of a client, and it is by one's particular skills, experiences and personal characteristics that one can become a successful temp. On the other hand, temping works by invoking a sense of competition, risk and urgency; that one can never be sure of one's position at the workplace, that one's competencies are always possible to replace, and that work is valorized according to a generalized market logic. In this way, temping aligns itself which a general organizational trait: that each position is independent of its occupant. As Ahrne (1994: 18) puts it, 'The recognition and identification of individual affiliates is indispensable for the running of an organization. Still, for the organization to last and survive no affiliate can be indispensable' (see Selznick 1948: 25). In this sense, organizations, temporary employment agencies and client organizations alike, both presuppose and transcend individual actors. This tension between uniqueness and substitutability characterizes the experiences of temps in Leeds, Santa Clara and Stockholm alike.

A large proportion of Swedish people will recall the massive marketing campaign launched by Teamwork/Manpower in the 1990s: 'Nisse from Manpower' ('Nisse från Manpower' in Swedish).[2] The campaign ran on television and radio for an extended period of time, and Nisse, the reliable substitute, came to be a well-known figure among the Swedish public. The message in the commercial spots was all the same: that every individual, no matter how well educated or high in the organizational hierarchy, can easily be substituted for. One example is the following:

(The phone rings)

> *Secretary*: Party Office
> *Conservative Party Leader*: Hi there, it's me. As you can see, I'm extremely busy at the moment.
> *Secretary*: Yes, yes, we do understand.
> *Conservative Party Leader*: And that's why I have a discreet question. Whether I could be spared the Party Congress for some time to come.
> *Secretary*: Yes, no problem at all. Should we skip the Committee as well?
> *Conservative Party Leader*: Yes, why not?
> *Secretary*: Mm. And the party leader debate?

> *Conservative Party Leader*: Well, let's not exaggerate. I am, after all, the leader of one of the biggest political parties in the country.
> *Secretary*: No worries, Nisse will deal with it.
> *Conservative Party Leader*: Well, Nisse, who's that?
> *Secretary*: Nisse from Teamwork. Clever guy. Popular.
> *Conservative Party Leader*: Actually, I don't think this is a very good idea. Do you know why?
> *Secretary*: No.
> *Conservative Party Leader*: I don't think it's good for Sweden. Really.
> (Jingle)
> *Voice-over*: When you want to recruit or lease competent personnel, call Teamwork!

The marketing campaign shows the frailty of individual actors' positions within the organizational landscape and in the labour market. Since there are substitutes out there, the organization is in a strong position to negotiate and define the terms for individual access to organizational resources and affiliation. The campaign shows the corporate power involved here – a power which claims to set the context for individual aspirations and imaginations and to decide on the nature of the contract between the individual and the organization. The campaign also fuels a strong sense of competition. Regardless of whether one is a temp or a regular, one cannot count on one's position being secure for ever. Rather, one needs to demonstrate commitment and competence to be continuously employable. The message of the campaign is that workmates today are more competitors than colleagues, and that the market has a role to play in who gets the upper hand. Be prepared!

Now, whilst there is much to suggest that temps themselves have taken in this competitive message, there is also evidence to the contrary.

Amanda, in Stockholm, has this story to tell:

> I am in a bit of a sensitive situation since I am replacing Jessie who is on sick leave. And she is in treatment, on sick leave. And she is coming back. And she is one of the team. And I don't want to replace her. That's why I keep a bit of a distance, so they don't think I'm trying to take her place. It's also out of respect for her.

So that she can feel when she is here that it's really her job. So I try not to change too much. She says I can, but I know what it feels like. If I move things around on her table and that. Of course it feels…. And then it's important that I don't socialize too much. Still, it's important that you try to become one among the team when you are here on a longer assignment.

Colleagues, competitors and clients

With spatial mobility and flexible contracts, work relations are made more episodic and a short-term mentality becomes the norm. Temps are rarely willing to invest in their colleagues at the agency, few of whom they know anyway, nor are they willing to invest in their clients, since these are, after all, only clients and, moreover, the assignment will sooner or later come to an end. We may describe ties in the blended workforce of temps and regulars as consisting of 'fleeting forms of association' (Sennett 1998), short-term cultures marked by 'the strength of weak ties', and not by loyalty or long-term relationships. 'There is little chance for mutual loyalty and commitment to sprout up and take root', as Bauman has it (2001: 25).

The forms of togetherness that characterize the blended workforce, that is, a workforce of both temporaries and regulars, can be understood as a 'tempered togetherness'. This is a deliberate togetherness, where staying together is done for the purpose of reaching a particular goal. 'Such togetherness', Bauman writes (1995: 46), 'is a matrix of (and for) structured encounters – normatively regulated, rule-governed, pre-emptively circumscribed and preferably sharp and short, lest they should spill over other encounters which need to be kept in a different register, lose focus, or grow receptive to purposes other than the one at hand.'

A recurring characteristic of work relations in such blended workforces is that the notion of 'colleague' itself becomes highly problematic.[3] When asked about this issue, temps often express uncertainty about who their 'real colleagues' are. As Maria at Olsten in Stockholm says:

Right now, I feel as though my colleagues are here, at the client's. But then there are also other consultants at the office, and staff, that I sometimes meet, and that I know, and they are also my colleagues. But there are also consultants that I don't know the name of, and they are in fact my colleagues as well. But right now my colleagues are here, at Ericsson [client's name, my insertion].

The above synthesizes a common reaction to the complexity of the colleague–client relationship as experienced by temps. Especially when temps are on long-term assignments, categories begin to blur and the client eventually becomes something of a colleague. This is often viewed as problematic, since temps are not supposed to engage with the client in a way that would complicate the professional relationship between service provider and service user. At the client's workplace, most temps prefer to keep a distance from their workmates, since they prefer to focus on the task at hand and not get too involved. Moreover, the agency recommends that they avoid taking part in gossip or talking behind people's backs at the client's.

As we discuss the issue of collegiality further, many temps begin to hesitate. A typical response would go like this:

But wait a second... my workmates here are actually my clients.... My colleagues, real colleagues, are the other temps who work for Olsten. But I hardly know who they are, or what they think, what their experiences are.

The communal aspect of work is undermined by continuous movement across client organizations as well as by the fact that assignments are by nature temporary. Temps experience a lack of collegial community. Concepts such as colleague, competitor and client are often vague and interchangeable. A temp's interest in getting to know one's temp colleagues is scant, since they will rarely end up working within the same client organization anyway. Interest in participating in social events organized by the temp agency is low, since they hardly know anyone among those who might attend. Their shared interests never coalesce into concerted action of any kind. The trade unions have very little impact on the formation of interest groupings. There is, even in Sweden where union membership is generally higher, a striking lack of knowledge regarding what the backing of a union or collective bargaining might bring about for them as individuals, and even less about what it might entail for them as a collectivity. 'The union .... I don't really know what it could do for me ' is a common expression when temps are asked about the role of the union in the temporary staffing business.

There is also the feeling that other temp colleagues are simultaneously one's competitors, competing for the appreciation of agency staff, for good assignments and for wages. This is also nurtured in by the continuous giving of awards and the media coverage given to 'The temp of the Month', 'the Golden Ant', or others who have made an outstanding contribution.

Temps at Olsten share, however, the concern of developing and maintaining good relations with the coordinators at the office during assignments, since being known and appreciated helps them get the next, and perhaps a more fulfilling, assignment. Temps on assignment need to keep this link back to the temp agency office alive in order to communicate how the assignment is working out and to increase their chances of an interesting next assignment. They know that their relationship with the agency needs to be nurtured through frequent contact and communication (also noted by Henson 1996: 65). The connection to the assignment coordinator is, in many ways, the lifeline between the employee and employer. In distributed forms of work, such as temping, personal connections are vital and the networks need to be constantly nurtured. This lifeline, or elastic band, between the agency and the temp may be constantly stretched, but should not break.

However, temps rarely feel that they communicate with the organization as a whole, that is, the temp agency, but rather with their own particular contact person. Hence, relations between employer and employee are strongly personalized and dependent on making a good personal connection. Contact is most often maintained through telephone calls, and the frequency with which temps call their contact person varies a great deal. While some would call a few times a week, others would only do so after the first day of the assignment, and when the assignment is coming to a close.

The shadow side of the emphasis on personal, rather then organizational, connection was also made clear in interviews with people who had previously been working as temps, but who had terminated their relation with the agency for different reasons. Some of them had not been offered the kinds of assignments they had hoped for; others had found a permanent job through the assignment; some could not cope with the stress of changing workplaces and workmates continuously; and yet others had never established a good relation with the assignment coordinator. Annica, in Stockholm, claimed the assignment coordinator never bothered to understand her skills, her goals or her personality. Hence, she got only 'the boring assignments'. After three months, she quit, without having secured another job. 'I just didn't see my future with Olsten', she explained.

The fluid or frail nature of work relations was also seen to carry certain advantages, however. The increased interlocking of networks and organizations across organizations can provide a resource of great significance for individuals in a competitive labour market. Networking across the boundaries of colleague, client and competitor increases the chances of achieving relevant information and of staying 'employable'. It is through the establishment of good social relations with workmates at the client's workplace and with assignment coordinators at the agency that the temporary employees are able to secure future assignments and make a career out of temping. Good relations with the assignment coordinator can also serve to cushion or smooth down complaints from grumpy clients or reduce the significance of a poor evaluation.

Also, collegial relations with other temporary employees, even though they are also recognized as competitors, are at times valuable for airing common concerns and interests, and hence, for a degree of community to arise – at least temporarily.

The idea of the self-sufficient individual, self-contained and self-moving, is a powerful factor in the organization of flexible labour markets. With conceptions of the self-sufficient individual go perceptions of the world. As Calhoun (1995: 254) puts it, 'Modern individualism ... is tied to distinctive conceptions of the world, conceptions that abandon the notion of an implicate order or encompassing hierarchy as the basic source of identity.'

The temporariness of assignments and relations in the workplace is a powerful individualizing force. It challenges the development of a sense of community, of common interest and loyalty. It makes the building of strong social ties difficult or uninteresting. The idea of 'common interests' is at risk of becoming nebulous and in the end incomprehensible (cf. Bauman 2001: 24–25).

Just a temp: On stigmatization

In some cases, the categorization of temps and regulars also involves stigmatization. Stigma draws a line between the two categories, accentuating attributed characteristics. More than once, I have come across the expression 'just a temp' in conversations with both temps and regulars.[4] The expression is a clear example of how the temp, despite all the empowering rhetoric, is degraded and made inferior in some way to the regular. Daniel Pink, in *Free Agent Nation* (2001), makes the distinction between 'high-end' temps and 'low-end temps'. Low-end temps' are the temps who do boring work for meagre pay in sometimes grim conditions. They are 'temp slaves', with no security and no respect. 'Temp slaves' frequently report being treated as some-how less than human because of their status in the workplace (2001: 215–216). In the worst workplaces 'temp slaves' become 'non-persons' in Goffman's sense (1959) – people who are sometimes treated in their presence as if they were not there.

Some of the temps I interviewed in Stockholm, Leeds and Santa Clara reported on being stigmatized as 'just a temp' and how this entailed not being included in social events, not being invited to join colleagues going out to lunch, and not being considered a reliable source of infor-mation. On occasion, they were used as scapegoats for things that had gone wrong, regardless of whether the mishap was their fault or not. The reason for this, according to the temps, was the ease with which regulars could escape responsibility and conflict simply by blaming someone who would in any case not be there for very long.

This excerpt from an interview with Emily, one of the Santa Clara temps, tells about the substitutability of temps as well as of the scape-goating that can sometimes be involved:

My friend, who works as a temp as well, tells me she feels a lot like, 'Well, I'm just the temp.' It's the attitude the client has. This is a risk for companies using temp agencies, I think. It's very difficult. ... Often the first day is when they get sent back. That, that very day. I had a position in a company that had a lot of complaints. Actually, I arrived as the second temp that day. The Olstens had sent a lady down. And this lady had basically not got along at all with the company. I don't know for what reason but when I arrived I didn't know this. And I walked into the little reception area and it was this terrible atmosphere and this woman was basically getting off her seat and she was storming out and she said to me, 'Well, I hope you have more luck than I did.' And she was really angry, and obviously they had a very bad impression of the temp and Olsten and they were sending me down. I think it was my first job. And I walked into this situation thinking, 'Oh, my goodness, they must, they'll hate me. They're looking for somebody else to find fault with.' So, I was extra specially polite, but they were cool towards me.

According to Pink, the stigmatization of temps has spawned a variety of responses from temps, one of which is a thriving, often underground, network of zines (self-published magazines), web sites, and popular culture expressions of discontent, let alone a new vocabulary for disgruntled temps (2001: 217). Likewise, Henson (1996: 145) says that

When temporary workers interact with others who perceive them as temporaries, they are confronted with their deviance. Temporaries cannot simply ignore the stigma of their imputed social identity. Like other stigmatized groups, temporaries can either internalize the stigma, incorporate it into their self-concept, or adopt strategies to deny, deflect, or manage it (Goffman 1961, 1963, Scott 1969).

Stigmatization uses attributes to establish relationships and to define proper and improper relations across the lines (Goffman 1963: 3, Tilly 1995: 65). Regulars aiming for upward mobility in the organization often make sure they do not socialize too much with temps, since these are of little value for their future career opportunities, and temps are generally regarded as occupying the lower rungs of the ladder. Rather, they tend to spend more time networking with other regulars whom they reckon to be of more importance to them in the future. Such strategic networking is both an expression of the stigmatization involved in the categorical relationship of temps and regulars and serves to further accentuate internal boundary lines. Again, such dramatic cases of categorization may persist for longer or shorter periods of time and may be more or less socially shared in the workplace. They are not absolute. That categories are negotiated in social interaction also means that they may be put to use situationally and strategically depending on the interests of the actors. Several informants have underlined the complexity of the temp–regular relationship, arguing that temps do not always and in all situations count as a given identity with particular characteristics associated with it. In the view of a manager at a client organization, 'There is also a difference between temps and temps.'

The tendency to refer to temps in a stigmatizing manner may be related to the temp being in a sense 'betwixt and between' organizational structures, 'neither here, nor there' (Garsten 1999). It is also to do with the imaginations and hopes that temps themselves bring to work, that temping can provide an alternative to the regular career-oriented job, that it is in some ways a 'job-not', (as discussed in Chapter 2). Despite the growing prevalence of short-term, contingent and non-standard contracts, temping is still in many ways a liminal type of employment relation, something that temps now and then experience in their social relations.

Localizing vagabonds: Brown bag luncheons and angel calls

Temping is largely done in a changing landscape of organizations, teams and workmates. The relative stability is not primarily to be found at the level of place, or locality, but rather in the array of transferable knowledge, skills and scripts. In a phrase that is reminiscent of Bauman's (2001: 25), one of my informants told me her place of work often felt like a camping site which one visits for a few nights only and which one may leave at any one time. In view of the continuous movement, the creation of 'local neighbourhoods' and of 'local subjects' is a perpetually ongoing project, to use Appadurai's terminology. Local knowledge may be understood as knowledge about how to create and recreate locality under conditions of social unrest, fragmentation and change, and uncertainty about how other people in one's proximity may act (Appadurai 1996: 181). Local knowledge is not primarily about narrow perspectives and being embedded in the here and now, but about creating reliable 'local subjects' and reliable' local neighbourhoods' within which such subjects may be recognized and organized.

This conjuring of a local 'we' comes into play in various ways. The local agencies do their best to attract the temps to the local office once in a while, for seminars, luncheons, meetings, parties and the like. They go to visit the temps at work in their different settings, or they call them on the phone to see how things are going. They provide them with gadgets that remind them of their connection to the local agency, such as pins, cups, calendars and the like. All in all, these relational mobilizations work to create a sense of local belonging and community. They also work to exercise a degree of control over a largely mobile and dispersed workforce.

The assignment coordinators at the Leeds office are very well aware of the many challenges of managing a contingent and mobile group of employees. It is all too easy, they explain, that as a temp, you start identifying with the employees of the client organization and their workplace, so that you forget where you belong. It is important that the temps can come to the temp agency office to meet their colleagues, to be reminded where they belong. The office staff think it is important that 'their' 'temps feel a certain belonging to the organization, not least in order to represent the agency well at the client organization. By different means, they try to draw the temps to the agency office every now and then.

Perhaps the most important of these measures is the 'Brown Bag Lunch' that takes place every Friday. Temps are encouraged to visit 'their' local agency to meet with the assignment coordinators and their temp colleagues, have a lunch sandwich, and get their pay cheques. These luncheons are to remind them of their relation to the employer and to strengthen the emotional ties between them:

> Please DON'T forget to join us in the branch for a FREE bite to eat and a chat on FRIDAY lunchtime whenever you can – we always look forward to seeing you! ('Welcome to Office Angels')

Whilst the agency office is usually relatively quiet, at Friday lunchtime it is bursting with activity. Temps from near and far hurry in to get their pay cheques, to grab a sandwich bag and to exchange a few quick words with the staff and with other temps. They also take the opportunity to have a look at the information about courses, seminars or free assignments that is posted on the walls. For a short while, the office turns into a real meeting-place for the temps and the agency staff. However, there are always large numbers of temps who do not have the opportunity to leave their work or who prioritize other errands. The Friday luncheons at the

Office Angels premises in Leeds are examples of the continuous making and remaking of a spatially grounded sense of community in translocal fields. The imagined and dispersed community that Olsten is also has to be localized in space where the core of the community can be expressed and where a sense of belonging can be created.

Once in a while, the staff does so-called 'Angel Calls' at the client organizations in which they have temps on assignments. This means they come to visit without any advance notice, to check up on their temps and to maintain good relations with the client. If there is a holiday coming up, they often bring chocolate, fruit or something similar: a symbolic gift. Many temps appreciate such tokens from the employer and think it contributes to strengthening the ties to the employer. Others regard it as an unnecessary control mechanism. In any case, the 'Angel Calls' are a way for the actors of the centre to engage with the periphery, so to speak.

Angel Calls are in no way specific to the Leeds office, but something that is undertaken in Santa Clara as well as in Stockholm, and that is practised in other temporary staffing companies as well.[5] Assignment coordinators in Santa Clara spend a considerable amount of time visiting with their temps throughout the Silicon Valley area. This is important, they consider, for maintaining the network of contacts with clients, for checking up on their temps, and for maintaining good relations with them.

In Stockholm, too, temps are reminded of the importance of maintaining close contact with the agency office:

> We think it is important to keep in touch with you during your assignments. During your employment with us you will be invited to open house, parties, or for a coffee in company with your colleagues at Olsten. We will also call you when you work at our clients' to make sure everything is working and that you are happy. ('A job to love')

Olsten organizes social events, such as after-work get-togethers, Christmas parties, summer parties and the like, to create a sense of belonging. Many of the Olsten temps think the social events organized by the agency are rather boring, since they have relatively little in common with other temps, and hardly even recognize them.

Eva, a well-experienced woman who works for Olsten in Stockholm, talks in length about what she thinks is a poor community feeling at Olsten:

> I know that Teamwork [another temporary staffing company] has breakfast meetings once in a while. Because they know people are working. It was easier for us to come by at 7.30 a.m. Have some morning coffee and chat with other temps. But with Olsten there are more meetings around classes and such. But we only have like six open positions for those. Tuesday, Wednesday, Thursday. And then they have evening opening hours. I have heard of other colleagues who have gone in.... They have arrived and then there was no one there. From the district. And they came in only for that! Because is says 'Open House. Come and have a chat and a bun!' ... So, it doesn't really work. There's a poor sense of community. You feel a little left out. Because you are all on your own out there. The only colleague I know is the girl who was here before me, whom I replaced, and who taught me. And the girl whom I taught and who replaced me when I was on holiday. And who will be here when I go on summer vacation. Those are the two I know.

At Olsten, the local place of belonging is not something that comes naturally, so to speak. Rather, agency staff have to work actively and continuously to make the temps feel that they are part of an organization with its own distinctive unity and culture. By attracting the temps to the centre of the dispersed network, to the agency premises, they attempt to make them feel at home and part of the community of Olsten employees. This works only to a limited extent, however, to give temporary recognition and a feeling of belonging.

Flexible employment, with its built-in mobility, challenges conventional organizational structures and the established forms of regulation and control that characterize regular, full-time employment. The spatial distance between the temp and the central agency worksite calls forth new strategies for regulation and control that differ from those in place in more stable and densely localized worksites. These spatial particularities transform authority relations and shape the type of control that the temp agency is able to exert over the temporary employee. These new types of control rely on decentring regulation and dispersing responsibility for control (cf. Gottfried 1992: 448), so that control is exercised from a distance, so to speak, through detailed norms and expectations, as well as through individuals themselves becoming 'responsible' and 'disciplined'.

Given the dispersed character of temp work, agencies face the challenge not only of control but also of creating a sense of belonging to the central location of the organization, that is, to the local agency office. Temporary employees have to be continuously reminded of their connections to the agency, of being agency representatives. They need to be reminded of the commitment and loyalty expected of them, and to be made reliable in the eyes of agency staff. Flexible regulation thus involves inventing ways of dealing with the particular spatialities of work in a way that maintains a sense of boundary, in the face of dispersed work practices and locations.

When physical monitoring is difficult, due to lack of spatial proximity, the creation of the sense of belonging, of community and commitment, becomes all the more important. Temps are induced to think about their local agency and their temp colleagues as part of the same cultural collectivity, and to recognize their similarities. The notion of an Olsten culture, however fluid, that is distinct from that of other temporary staffing companies, is nurtured to foster allegiance and trust. However, as we have seen, it is a culture that relies not so much on shared and taken-for-granted values and perspectives, as it does on transferable skills, selves and scripts. Yet, the conjuring of a local 'we' contributes to facilitating the substitutability of affiliates. It helps to socialize new recruits and provides a way to refer to the Olsten temp agency as 'different' from other organizations.

Concluding discussion: The frailty of transorganizational work communities

The discontinuity of flexible work operates not only at the spatial and temporal level, but also at the social, community level. This means that the kinds of communities we see in places where temporary workers are numerous tend to be quite contingent and fragile. This is not to say that they may not be intense or deep during the time they are working and socializing together, but that discontinuity shapes the notion of community in a certain direction, towards more fluidity and sweeping engagement than long-term investment in collegial relations.

In a general sense, organizing is a struggle for control and order, an attempt to make sense of and to rationalize environments, and eventually to reduce uncertainty. Work organizations are structured so as to gain control over the production process as well as over employees. Spatial proximity and ordering of work groups, a careful physical layout of the facilities, as well as the rational physical ordering of the work process have been crucial in this process. In Chapter 2, I described Olsten as a translocality, shot through with the movement of people, products, ideas, knowledge and the like. Temporary employment agencies reveal a lower sense of coherence than what is normally attributed to organizations. They are to a large extent distributed across space, and contract and expand more easily than many other types of business organizations. From the viewpoint of managerial control, organizational norms need also to be encouraged to go beyond the workplace. The meaning of the boundary of the organization is thus in a sense re-organized to stretch outside the premises of the temporary staffing organization (cf. Fleming 2004).

There is ample evidence to suggest that temps contribute to knitting organizational structures more tightly together by challenging and transcending organizational boundaries. They bring in a greater degree of complexity to established organizational structures. They introduce alternative organizational forms and alternative ways of relating to work and employment. Temporaries may act as mediators and transformers between organizations, distributing and 'creolizing' information and knowledge (Hannerz 1987). We have also witnessed how boundary-spanning work practices lead to the blurring of established social distinctions between 'colleagues', clients' and 'competitors'. However, flexible work arrangements also contribute to the establishment of new kinds of organizational boundaries. Flexible work may lead to the establishment of new forms of inequality between so-called 'regulars' and temps. Boundary-breaking and boundary-making thus go hand in hand.

It is important here to recognize the normative and postulated in these kinds of work communities. 'Local neighbourhoods' and 'local subjects' are not given, but 'made up' as part of the effort to gain a degree of control and instil a degree of commitment to the organization. In a similar vein of thought Casey (1996) argues that the new corporate culture currently being constructed in new forms of work has wide social implications. She argues that the deliberate reconstruction of corporate culture involves the construction of a corporate 'designer culture', a simulated culture that requires and produces a shift in employee identification and solidarities. This post-industrial, 'post-occupational' social solidarity also involves the fashioning of a new subjectivity for the 'designer employee', she suggests. The evocative notion of 'designer culture' has a strong bearing also on temps, since it brings to the fore the conscious moulding of a postulated kind of community.

The social life of temps, as for all employees of complex organizations, involve a variety of shifts between types of relations; direct face-to-face meetings, mediated encounters, relations of surveillance and control, as well as intimate togetherness. Temping life is multi-faceted in terms of the amount of different social relations that can be experienced and established. But the directionality and durability of the relations is always controlled by the temp agency and the contact that is set up with client organizations.

7
Renderings: Fragments of Freedom

Being flexible – can we conceive of this stance as a blueprint for a desired life and form of work? Flexibility comes with a bundle of positive imaginings attached to it: freedom, empowerment, dynamism. It also comes with a set of requests for less attractive notions: preparedness, adaptation and regulation. Somewhere in-between, flexible employees have to find their feet and construct their own worklives.

These worklives are subject to transnational influences, shaped by globalization of organizations and labour markets, flexibilization of organizational forms and labour markets and knowledge-intensive production mediated through large-scale temporary staffing agencies. In this process of changing employment relations and organizational forms, the employees of tomorrow are up against the challenge of constructing a sense of career and community out of their work assignments. This involves dealing with the volatility of work contracts and organizations, the uncertainties of work assignments, and the risks of competitive labour markets. It also entails adopting a reflexive stance towards one's prospects and opportunities. Employees in the new worlds of work have to draw on a portfolio of different skills, professional as well as social, and to be able to adapt to different circumstances as they arise.

The case of temporary employees speaks to larger trends in the transformation of labour markets by highlighting and bringing into focus experiences that will affect many of us. To a great extent, the notion of 'workplace vagabonds' evokes skills, competencies and social traits that will become characteristic not only of temporary employees but also of a large portion of the labour force. Experiences gained from flexible work put old, institutionalized patterns of thought and action into question and give rise to new perspectives and ways of acting. It is within this dynamic context of interacting perspectives that the workplace vagabonds construct their understandings of career and community.

The agentic employee

In this new workscape, we are seeing a gradual shift of regulatory initiative and capacity from state level to private and to supranational regulators of various kinds, be they corporations, international organizations or multilateral organizations (cf. Sassen 1998, Rosenau 2003). An important aspect of this process is that individuals emerge as regulatory sites. The individual becomes a focal point for regulatory intervention, and the burden of responsibility for worklife and career is placed onto the individual. These new regulatory forms often supersede the state level and take on voluntary and subtle forms, but they may be extremely powerful and influential in character. The individual faces new social techniques of control and normative influences, which fashion action and thinking in a particular direction (Garsten and Jacobsson 2004).

Alongside the structural fragmentation of work arrangements, the vocabularies of flexibility, employability and lifelong learning also work to individualize and to fragment the collective fabric of worklife. People who occupy temporary, flexible jobs are met with the notion that the principal actors in organizations, in the labour market, indeed in the economy and society at large, are individuals. Temping is, in a sense, the ultimate expression of individualized potentiality and power. It sets you free, whilst also demanding self-reliance and 'responsibilization', or so the talk goes. It is positioned as a voluntary undertaking, and so, what you make out of it is entirely up to you. It takes discipline and self-management.

The forms of regulation and control that appear in the flexible work industry rely on the assumption of an 'exaggerated actorhood', to use Meyer and Jepperson's expression (2000). Much social theory of contemporary work and labour markets takes for granted 'the core conceit of modern culture, that modern actors – individuals, organizations, nation states – are autochthonous and natural entities, no longer really embedded in culture', as Meyer and Jepperson have it (2000: 100). In the flexible labour market, temps are constructed as authorized agents for various interests. This authorized agentic capability as an essential feature of what modern theory and culture call an 'actor', and one that, when analysed, illuminates a number of otherwise forgotten or hidden features of the workings of modern individuals, organizations and states. These include the diffusion of scenarios of imaginations and expectations, of normative ideas, of practices of evaluation, and their limited capacity for prolific collective action (cf. Meyer and Jepperson 2000: 100).

When seen from this perspective, we may understand that the free agent ideology of flexible temporary work is crucial in making work appear as individualized, fragmented and disconnected, and that this is, in fact, part of the way in which flexibility as a regulatory mechanism works. The forms of regulation and control that are developed in flexible, temporary work are dependent upon the notion of the individual agent, of self-reliance and self-governance, in order to function properly as such.

The perceptions of market rationality that are at work in flexible labour markets celebrate a particular version of the agentic, self-reliant individual. We see this operating in Sweden as well as in the UK and the US, but it seems to go particularly well with American cultural templates of the hero. Indeed, as Ong (2006: 159) asserts, with special reference to knowledge-based jobs:

> [T]o be American is to be self-reliant, self-empowering, and tech-nologically savvy, qualities that ensure access to college education and a comfortable middle-class life, with all its accoutrements. We have long admired heroes with scientific talent – say, the astro-naut Neil Armstrong, or the discoverers of the DNS, James Watson and Francis Crick – though lately the celebrities have tended to be the cyberheroes such as Steve Jobs (and entrepreneurs such as Donald Trump).

The political vocabulary of flexibility promises a new identity for the individual and gives rise to new strategies of governing the work-place, in which order is to be achieved through individuals improv-ing and disciplining themselves, to become entrepreneurial, flexible, employable and self-sufficient members of society. In this process, a new set of political and well as employee ideals are articulated. The values of autonomy, entrepreneurship and self-motivation are highlighted, aligning ideals of individualism to neoliberal political visions.

The standardized making of individual performers

Flexibility is a double-edged sword; while it is understood to mean the loosening of rules, and adaptation to unique, local conditions, it also entails the putting into place of new, alternative rules to govern the individual, with universalistic claims. It entails the capacity to bend, to adapt, to be attentive to manners and attitudes, in order to be 'flexible', and hence 'employable'. While certain aspects of individual ideas, attitudes and actions are rendered normal and indeed wanted, others are muted.

Flexibility brings with it new ways of governing the individual. It points to a tension between subjective control of one's work trajectory on the one hand and the framework provided by the temporary employment agency and the client organization on the other. The practices that are put in place entail, in other words, a tension between the individual's perceptions and preferences and those of the organization. Whilst flexibilization would at first glance appear to be in stark contrast with anything that leads in the direction of rigidity, structure, standardization and the like, the case is not as simple as that. In flexible work, the individualization of risk goes hand in hand with a social construction of a collective category of workers – the flexible temps – where the procedures of being employed, assigned work and evaluated involve new patterns of regulation and governance.

For temps, everyday worklife is saturated with rules, norms and belief systems that undergird the social and organizational structures of work. As we have seen in this book, there are rules for how to behave on your first day of a new assignment, how to dress properly, and what criteria to pay attention to in evaluation procedures. The abundance of voluntary rules, enforced through the mobilization of responsibility, takes on an unprecedented significance in environments where uncertainty and risk prevail, and where a shared consensus as to what rules are at work and what assumptions are shared cannot be taken for granted (Brunsson and Jacobsson 2000).

These rules come in the form of policies, norms, advice and rewards, and hence constitute a 'soft' means of governing the individual. They contribute to the fostering of flexibility 'by aspiration'. By no means does this mean that they are weaker in the way they work. On the contrary, they may be just as hard in their consequences as are directives. The arrangement of these rules works to encourage and maintain the idea that flexibility is a potential for the individual to be explored, rather than adapted to. It works to instil a sense of agency and responsibility on the part of individuals, who learn to take upon themselves the risks and opportunities that await them. Tuning into aspirations of agency and freedom are part and parcel of the governance of flexible workers. We should be careful, however, not to accept uncritically the idea of individuals as autonomous agents. Temporary employees, like other social actors, are tightly entangled in the wider structures and forces that influence and respond to their own ideas and actions. The agentic capacity of temps is fraught with the frictions that emerge at the junctures of market rationality, organizational logics and a set of cultural assumptions.

The agency's claim to have influence over a temp's physical appearance, manners and emotional display is backed up by the continuous reference to the need to represent the agency professionally and to accommodate to the client's expectations. This is a market demand to which individuals have to adapt flexibly. Developing a repertoire of transferable skills, showing the right attitude and dressing properly is part of what it takes to be flexible. However contradictory it may seem, being flexible thus involves accepting the rules of standardization (cf. Hochshild 1983: 103).

By linking flexibility to standardization of patterns of thought and action, the agency can control aspects of the temps' behaviour that they would otherwise not be able to, given their spatial dispersal and mobility. The more precarious the temp–agency relationship, the larger the scope for control of the temporary agency worker's display of attitude, appearance and manners. The more frail the employment relationship, the stronger the normative charge in the corporate culture programmes and technologies.

In the whirlpool

I have suggested that people who are part of the new, mobile and temporary workforce pay a lot of attention to reflexive thinking about how to enhance their skills, the ways in which they relate to the client, the kinds of emotions and attitudes they display, and their appearance (cf. Rogers 1995, Henson 1996, Hochschild 1983). This is seen by many as a career strategy – as a way to increase the chances of getting new, more advanced and more stimulating assignments, and of achieving a meaningful worklife.

Reflexivity is also intimately related to the development of work community, since flexible work arrangements force individuals to continuously reflect and act upon their involvements with colleagues in different work settings. The temporary and purpose-oriented nature of work relations means that relations cannot be taken for granted and left to evolve spontaneously, but have to be more consciously enacted and maintained. This involves the construction of similarities and differences, the accentuation of particular traits of character, skills, norms and so on, and the downplaying of others.

This reflexivity entails learning to be sensitive to the ways of the market. Notions of flexibility, enterprise culture and so on lead us to see the extent to which the market is becoming a mobilizing metaphor in the 'making up' of individuals in the labour market. Temps, as typecasts of *homo mercans* (Garsten 2002, Garsten and Hasselström 2004), learn to orient themselves towards market transactions. They are meshed into a competitive culture that places prime value on the marketability of goods and services as well as skills, competences, manners and attitudes. They learn to think in terms of valuation and evaluation, to value themselves as 'products' in the market, to make themselves auditable, and to take on the idea of enterprise as a mode of action. Moreover, they are taught to see themselves as autonomous, self-reliant and disciplined. Generally, there is in the business the assumption that the sort of person contained in the market model is the true or valid person, the standard against which other notions of the self are measured, and usually found wanting (cf. Carrier 1997). In a somewhat condensed version, the idea is that it is possible, through education, corporate cultural change programmes, reward systems and technologies, to get people to accept and integrate the workings of the market as given. In a Foucauldian view, to be market-oriented is, in the conception of the new global economy, the normal way of being. And it is partly through such notions and requests that the new forms of governance and power operates: 'The process of normalization lies at the heart of how modern power operates: the 'normalizing gaze...establishes over individuals a visibility through which one differentiates them and judges them' (Foucault 1991).

In contemporary labour markets, emerging divisions are now increasingly made up by differential access to unpredictability, and hence to freedom (cf. Bauman 2000: 120). Mobility or rather, the control over mobility, has become a key stratifying factor (Bauman 1998a: 9, Chapter 4). Mobility distributes people into new kinds of hierarchies, constitutes the individual work identity and contributes to the development of a particular type of 'market discipline'. The character of work and the degrees of control over spatial mobility that one's position entails also inform the kinds of perspectives that are revealed in relation to mobility. When high-flying management consultants travel between cities and clients, mobility has a different ring to it, is seen as more prestigious and glamorous, at least from the outside. An agenda filled with destinations near and far symbolizes a certain amount of cultural capital, to use Bourdieu's terms (1984). While consultants tend to 'travel', temps tend to 'jump around'.

Entangled with the spatial patterning of flexible work are also the temporal aspects of work. Being in control of the duration of contracts, the speed with which work has to be done, and the general temporal mapping of work, provides a degree of privilege in relation to the situation of those whose time is being managed. Differential access to instantaneity, to speed and to movement defines to a large extent one's position in the flexible labour market.

Whilst flexibilization would at first glance appear to be in stark contrast with anything that leads in the direction of hierarchy and organization, the case is not as simple as that. Flexibilization goes hand in hand with the making of new boundaries in the workplace and the masking of hierarchy and organization by individualizing practices that are, somewhat paradoxically, organized. These larger structures of organization interact in sophisticated ways with people's imaginations, actions and everyday worklives.

Indeed, there is a sense in which even the ubiquitous discourse of flexibility and change actually betokens a kind of stability: precisely because it is so ubiquitous it offers a sense of security and even an identity based upon one's capacity to be flexible, to 'ride the waves of change' like a sort of organization surfer.

Notes

Introduction: Changing Worlds of Work

1. Olsten later merged with Adecco, a Swiss-based multinational temporary help agency.
2. The research project has been financially supported through research grants from the Swedish Research Council and the Swedish Council for Working Life and Social Research.
3. The case material provided builds primarily on around 30 interviews with temps and staff at Olsten Corporation in Sweden, 40 interviews in Santa Clara county, California, and 30 in Leeds, UK, during the period 1996–1999. I also did around 10 interviews with people who had previously been working as temps, but who had terminated their relation with the agency for various reasons.

1 Work in the Global Economy

1. While globalization is often seen as driven by large-scale corporations and other transnational organizations, enterprises operated by petty capitalists also play important roles in the global economic development. Smart and Smart (2005) show how small firms are mobilizing to compete in a global economy, and that there is nothing petty about their significance for understanding contemporary economy, society and culture.
2. Indeed, there are many varieties of flexibility. Usually, 'numerical' or 'external' flexibility refers to the fluctuations in workforce numbers according to demand; 'functional' or 'internal' flexibility connotes the adaptability of skilled workers to utilize a wide range of skills; 'temporal' flexibility refers to varying patterns in working hours to reflect varying demand (Goudswaard and de Nanteuil 2000: 28).
3. Also set in the context of vibrant Silicon Valley, Benner (2002) offers a thorough analysis of the transformation of work, as shaped by demands for flexibility and through intermediaries, towards more tenuous and volatile contracts. The book examines the increasingly important role of labour market intermediaries, such as temporary staffing agencies, in a highly dynamic labour market. See also studies by Bergström and Storrie (2003), Furåker, Håkansson and Karlsson (2007), McAllister (1998), Parker (1994), Rogers (1995, 2000), Henson (1996), Smith (1998), Vosko (2000) and, from the Swedish context, Hanson (2004) and Walter (2005).
4. This section is built primarily around interviews with Olsten and Adecco managers, but also owes clarifying details to the Kedia and Tufano Harvard case study (2001).

5. For a more detailed account of the Swedish legislative structure in relation to temporary agency work, see Friberg et al. (1999), Furåker (2007).

6. Furthermore, with the State's abandonment of its earlier policy of granting temporary agency workers unemployment benefits between assignments, the agencies were recognized as employers who had to take full responsibility for their employees, instead of living off the hand-outs of the unions which were 'providing them with stock', as a representative of the Swedish Trade Union Confederation put it. Here the State could still to some extent function as a buffer against too much global market infiltration.

7. Personal communication with the Salaried Employees' Union, HTF, and the Swedish Association of Temporary Work Businesses and Staffing Services, SPUR, in September 2002.

8. The role of unions in lobbying, organizing and regulating the temporary agency market varies across the country contexts of this study. In general, the role of unions in Sweden has been quite strong, even though temporary agency workers are less unionized than the workforce at large. The US and UK represent significantly different cases, with unions being much weaker and workers most often non-unionized.

9. The debate on the 'feminization' of work is also one with global ramifications, and one which extends beyond temping and the labour market. See for example Calas and Smircich, (1993), Ferguson (1984) and Fondas (1993, 1996).

10. The staff 'headcount' of an organization is generally understood as the number of full-time person-years attributable to people who have worked within or for the organization during a year. So the contributions of those who work on a temporary basis count as appropriate fractions of a full-time person-year.

11. Generally, statistics on ethnic origin are difficult to find, and the information not always reported to investigating parties. Debates on this issue bring forward arguments that maintain the significant role that temporary agencies play in finding work for immigrants and people with ethnic origins that are other than the dominant ones in their area of work, on the one hand, and on the marginalizing effects that temporary work may have for some people, on the other. See, for example, Friberg et al. (1999) and Fridén et al. (2000) for some discussions around these issues in Sweden, Furåker et al. (2007) for the European context; and Kalleberg et al. (2000) for the US.

12. Supiot (2001) provides a broad overview of the transformation of European labour law more generally, which describes the background to recent changes in relation to temporary work.

13. See Ahrne, Göran, Nils Brunsson and Christina Garsten (2002) for a study of the Swedish branch organization SPUR, now the Swedish Association of Staff Agencies, as a 'meta-organization' involved in regulating the field.

14. There are plenty of contemporary debates trying to make sense of regulatory changes brought about by globalization. The re-thinking of

regulation is captured in phrases such as 'from government to governance', 'from deregulation to re-regulation', 'from hard to soft regulation' and a move towards 'new forms of governance'. These phrases point to shifts in the type and nature of regulation, as well as in the sets of actors involved. See, for example, Djelic and Sahlin-Andersson (2004), Hall and Biersteker (2002) and Strange (1996).

2 Into the Temping Zone

1. This is my translation of a Swedish staffing agency's advertising campaign that was run throughout Stockholm a couple of years ago.
2. All informants' quotations have been translated from Swedish to English by myself, as have Olsten documents in Swedish.
3. On the complex forms of regulation of benefits in the temporary staffing industry, see for example, Sweeney (2006).
4. See also, for example, D'Mello (2006), Fisher and Downey (2006), Hannerz (2004), Hasselström 2003, Riles (2000) and Wulff (1998) for other kinds of discontinuous ethnographic practices.

3 'Jumping Around': Translocal Movements

1. Birgitta Svensson also makes this point in her interesting study of 'travellers' (1993).
2. Haunschild (2003) shows how employment systems in the culture industry, more specifically for German theatre artists, are also marked by high labour mobility and contingent work arrangements, and where the ensemble structure provides (temporary) stability of the workforce.
3. See also Walter (2005) for a thorough discussion on the complexities of matching job assignments and candidates at a temp agency in Sweden.
4. There are numerous self-help books on how to manage in the competitive labour market, some of which cater explicitly to temporary agency work. And these are interesting reading. Written by people who have themselves worked in the temporary industry, or by consultants and career advisors who specialize in employment relations and career development, they provide you with ample advice and guidance as to how best to manage your career and optimize opportunities in the temp market.
5. A number of scholars have treated organizing and organizations from the dramaturgical perspective developed by Goffman (1974) or others, such as Burke (for example, 1972), Debord (1967), Boal (1979 [1974]) or Bahktin (1984). Among those who have contributed to understanding organizational life as 'theatrical' performance involving scripts are Czarniawska (1997), Kärreman (2001), Boje (1995, 2001) and Mangham (1990).

4 Just-in-Time: Temping Timelines and Time Tools

1. Thompson (1967), among others, has argued that the creation of, and internalization of, a time discipline among the workforce represented a key feature in the development of an urbanized, industrialized economy.
2. Micki McGee (1995) has written a captivating book on the self-help industry and makeover culture that she sees as taking a hold on American life. In this process, technologies for time management are also crucial.

5 Expectation and Evaluation

1. In a previous publication, I have described how temps are taught what it takes to be flexible as part of being 'employable', and the practices of evaluation used (Garsten 2004).
2. There is a certain plasticity involved here that brings to mind media characters with superhuman capacities, like Gumby, the Elastigirl, or the male version, Spiderman.
3. Writing about women workers in Silicon Valley, Karen Hossfeld (1990) describes how managers encourage forms of work culture that enhance conventional forms of femininity, involving expensive and time-consuming rituals of manicures, hair stylings and fashion.

6 Contingent Communities

1. A large body of research has contributed to the understanding of the role of 'work' as a social basis for the creation of a sense of identity, both individual and group identity, and of community. For an informative overview of central perspectives, see, for example, Noon and Blyton (1997) and Gamst (1995).
2. Teamwork, a Swedish temporary staffing company, was set up in 1953 and was acquired by Manpower in 1996.
3. I have also explored this aspect of temping in a previous publication, see Garsten (2003).
4. The expression 'just a temp' is not only commonly used among temps themselves, but has also inspired titles for academic works, for example Rogers (1995), Henson (1996), Casey and Alach (2004).
5. Funnily, in my role as Head of Department at Stockholm University, I have myself greeted calls from a temporary staffing company, who regularly sends one of their staff to visit the temp that works for us in our Student Reception.

References

Ackroyd, Stephen. 2007. Large corporations and the emergence of a flexible economic system: Some recent developments in the UK. In Bengt Furåker, Kristina Håkansson and Jan C. Karlsson, eds. *Flexiblity and Stability in Working Life*. Basingstoke: Palgrave Macmillan, pp. 83–102.

Ahrne, Göran. 1994. *Social Organizations: Interaction Inside, Outside and Between Organizations*. London: Sage.

Ahrne, Göran, Nils Brunsson and Christina Garsten. 2002 (2000). Standardizing through organization. In Nils Brunsson and Bengt Jacobsson, eds. *A World of Standards*. Oxford: Oxford University Press, pp. 50–70.

Albrow, Martin, John Eade, Jörg Durrschmidt and Neil Washbourne. 1997. The impact of globalization on sociological concepts. Community, culture and milieu. In J. Eade, ed. *Living the Global City*. London: Routledge, pp. 20–36.

Allen, John and Nick Henry. 1996. Fragments of industry and employment: Contract service work and the shift towards precarious employment. In Rosemary Crompton, Duncan Gallie and Kate Purcell, eds. *Changing Forms of Employment. Organisations, Skills and Gender*. London: Routledge, pp. 65–82.

Allvin, Michael. 2004. The individualization of labour. In Christina Garsten and Kerstin Jacobsson, eds. *Learning to be Employable: New Agendas on Work, Employability and Learning in a Globalizing World*. Basingstoke: Palgrave Macmillan, pp. 23–41.

Appadurai, Arjun. 1990. Disjuncture and difference in the global cultural economy. In Mike Featherstone, ed. *Global Culture: Nationalism, Globalization and Modernity*. London: Sage, pp. 295–310.

Appadurai, Arjun. 1996. *Modernity at Large*. Minneapolis: University of Minnesota Press.

Arthur, Michael B. and Denise M. Rousseau, eds. 1996. *The Boundaryless Career: A New Employment Principle for a New Organizational Era*. Oxford: Oxford University Press.

Barker, James R. 1999. *The Discipline of Teamwork: Participation and Concertive Control*. Thousand Oaks. CA: Sage.

Barley, Stephen R. and Gideon Kunda. 2001. Bringing work back in. *Organization Science*, 12(1): 76–95.

Barley, Stephen R. and Gideon Kunda. 2004. *Gurus, Hired Guns, and Warm Bodies: Itinerant Experts in a Knowledge Economy*. Princeton. NJ: Princeton University Press.

Bauman, Zygmunt. 1995. *Life in Fragments: Essays in Postmodern Morality*. Oxford: Blackwell.

Bauman, Zygmunt. 1998a. *Globalization: The Human Consequences.* New York, NY: Columbia University Press.

Bauman, Zygmunt. 1998b. *Work, Consumerism and the New Poor.* Buckingham: Open University Press.

Bauman, Zygmunt. 2000. *Liquid Modernity.* Cambridge: Polity Press.

Bauman, Zygmunt, 2001. *The Individualized Society.* Cambridge: Polity Press.

Benner, Chris. 2002. *Work in the New Economy: Flexible Labor Markets in the Silicon Valley.* Malden, MA: Blackwell.

Bergström, Ola and Donald Storrie, eds. 2003. *Contingent Employment in Europe and the United States.* Cheltenham: Edward Elgar.

Biao, Xiang. 2007. *'Body Shopping': An Indian Labor System in the Information Technology Industry.* Princeton, NJ: Princeton University Press.

Boal, Augusto. 1979 (1974). *Theatre of the Oppressed.* (O. Leal McBride, Trans.). Originally published in Spanish as *Teatro de Oprimido* (1974). New York, NY: Theatre Communications Group.

Boje, David M. 1995. Stories of the storytelling organization: A postmodern analysis of Disney as Tamara-land. *Academy of Management Journal,* 38(4): 997–1035.

Boje, David M. 2001. Carnivalesque resistance to global spectacle: A critical postmodern theory of public administration. *Administrative Theory and Praxis,* 23(3): 431–458.

Bourdieu, Pierre. 1984. *Distinction.* Cambridge, MA: Harvard University Press.

Brunsson, Nils, Bengt Jacobsson and associates. 2002 (2000). *A World of Standards.* Oxford: Oxford University Press.

Bureau of Labor Statistics. 2005. (http://www.bls.gov/news.release/pdf/conemp.pdf, visited 22 July 2007).

Burke, Kenneth. 1972. *Dramatism and Development.* Barre, MA: Clark University Press with Barre Publishers.

Calas, Marta B. and Linda Smircich. 1993. Dangerous liaisons: The 'feminine-in-management' meets globalization. *Business Horizons,* March–April: 71–81.

Calhoun, Craig. 1992. The infrastructure of modernity: Indirect social relationships, information technology, and social integration. In Hans Haferkamp and Neil J. Smelser, eds. *Social Change and Modernity.* Berkeley: University of California Press, pp. 205–236.

Calhoun, Craig. 1995. *Critical Social Theory: Culture, History, and the Challenge of Difference.* Oxford: Blackwell.

Carrier, James G. 1997. Introduction. In James G. Carrier, ed. *Meanings of the Market.* Oxford: Berg, pp. 1–67.

Casey, Bernard. 1987. *Temporary Employment: Practice and Policy in Britain.* London: Policy Studies Institute.

Casey, Catherine. 1996. Corporate transformations: Designer culture, designer employees and 'post-occupational' solidarity. *Organization,* 3(3): 317–339.

Casey, Catherine and Patricia Alach. 2004. 'Just a temp?' Women, temporary employment and lifestyle. *Work, Employment & Society,* 18(3): 459–480.

CEC [Commission of the European Communities]. 2002. *Proposal for a directive of the European Parliament and the Council on working conditions for temporary workers*, COM(2002)149 final.

Ciborra, Claudio. (2004 [2002]). *The Labyrinths of Information: Challenging the Wisdom of Systems*. Oxford: Oxford University Press.

CIETT. 2005. (International Confederation of Temporary Work Businesses) Agency Work Statistics. (http://www.ciett.org/fileadmin/templates/ciett/docs/CIETT_2005_Statistics.pdf, visited 20 July 2007)

Clegg, Stewart, Martin Kornberger and Tyrone Pitsis. 2005. *Managing and Organization: An Introduction to Theory and Practice*. London: Sage.

Cohen, Laurie and Mary Mallon. 1999. The transition from organisational employment to portfolio working: Perceptions of 'boundarylessness'. *Work, Employment & Society*, 13(2): 329–352.

Collin, Audrey. 2000. Dancing to the music of time. In Richard A. Young and Audrey Collin, eds. *The Future of Career*. Cambridge: Cambridge University Press, pp. 83–97.

Collin, Audrey and Richard Young. 2000. Introduction: Framing the future of career. In Richard A. Young and Audrey Collin, eds. *The Future of Career*. Cambridge: Cambridge University Press, pp. 1–20.

Collinson, David. 1987. Picking women: The recruitment of temporary workers in the mail order industry. *Work, Employment and Society*, 1(3): 371–387.

Czarniawska, Barbara. (1997). *Narrating the Organization: Dramas of Institutional Identity*. Chicago, IL: University of Chicago Press.

Czarniawska, Barbara. 2004. On time, space, and action *nets. Organization*, 6(11): 773–791.

Debord, Guy. 1967. *La Société du Spectacle*. Paris: Editions Buchet-Chastel. The full text is available at http://www.nothingness.org/SI/debord/index.html

Djelic, Marie-Laure and Kerstin Sahlin-Andersson, eds. 2004. *Transnational Governance: Institutional Dynamics of Regulation*. Cambridge: Cambridge University Press.

D'Mello, Marisa. 2006. *Understanding Selves and Identities of Information Technology Professionals. A Case Study from India*. Doctoral dissertation. Oslo: Centre for Technology, Innovation and Culture. Faculty of Social Sciences, University of Oslo.

du Gay, Paul. 1991. Enterprise culture and the ideology of excellence. *New Formations*, 13: 45–61.

du Gay, Paul. 1996. *Consumption and Identity at Work*. London: Sage.

European Foundation for Improvement of Living and Working Conditions. 2006. *Temporary agency work in an enlarged European Union*. (http://www.ciett.org/fileadmin/templates/ciett/research/EIRO_Foundation_report_on_TAW_-_March_01.pdf, visited 20 July 2007)

Fenton, Steve and Esther Dermott. 2006. Fragnebted Careers? Winners and losers in young adult labour markets. *Work, Employment & Society*, 20(2): 205–221.

Ferguson, Kathy E. 1984. *The Feminist Case Against Bureaucracy*. Philadelphia: Temple University Press.

Fineman, Steven, 2000. Emotional arenas revisited. In Stephen Fineman, ed. *Emotion in Organizations*. London: Sage, pp. 1–24.

Fisher, Melissa and Greg Downey, eds. 2006. *Frontiers of Capital: Ethnographic Reflections on the New Economy*. Durham, NC: Duke University Press.

Fleming, Peter. 2004. 'You can check out anytime, but you can never leave': Spatial boundaries in a high commitment organization. *Human Relations*, 57(1): 75–94.

Fondas, Nanette. 1993. The feminization of American management. In D. Moore, ed. *Academy of Management Best Paper Proceedings*. Altlanta, GA: Academy of Management, pp. 358–362.

Fondas, Nanette. 1996. Feminization at work: Career implications. In Michael B. Arthur, and Denise M. Rousseau, eds. *The Boundaryless Career. A New Employment Principle for a New Organizational Era*. New York, NY: Oxford University Press, pp. 282–293.

Forde, Chris. 1997. Temporary employment agency working: Issues and evidence. Paper presented for the 15th International Labour Process Conference, University of Edinburgh, 25–27 March, 1997.

Forde Chris. 2001. Temporary arrangements: The activities of employment agencies in the UK. *Work, Employment & Society*, 9(15): 631–644.

Foucault, Michel 1991. *Discipline and Punish: The Birth of the Prison*. Harmondsworth: Penguin.

Freeman, Carla. 2000. *High Tech and High Heels in the Global Economy: Women, Work and Pink-Collar Identities in the Caribbean*. Durham, NC: Duke University Press.

Friberg, Kent, Åsa Olli and Eskil Wadensjö. 1999. *Privat förmedling av arbete i Sverige: Konkurrens eller samarbete mellan offentlig och privat förmedlingsverksamhet*. Stockholm: Institute for Social Research (SOFI), Stockholm University.

Friden, Lennart, Ylva Hedén and Eskil Wadensjö. 2000. Personaluthyrningsföretag – en bro till arbetsmarknaden? (Appendix two to Diversity Project). Stockholm. Government Offices of Sweden. Ministry of Enterprise, Energy and Communications.

Furåker, Bengt. 1979. *Stat och arbetsmarknad. Studier i svensk rörlighetspolitik*. Lund: Arkiv avhandlingsserie.

Furåker, Bengt. 2007. Types of employment contract and attitudes to flexibility: An analysis of data from three Swedish surveys. In Bengt Furåker, Kristina Håkansson and Jan C. Karlsson, eds. *Flexiblity and Stability in Working Life*. Basingstoke: Palgrave Macmillan, pp. 173–196.

Furåker, Bengt, Kristina Håkansson and Jan C. Karlsson, eds. 2007. *Flexiblity and Stability in Working Life*. Basingstoke: Palgrave Macmillan.

Gamst, Frederick C., ed. 1995. *Meanings of Work: Considerations for the Twenty-First Century*. Albany, NY: State University of New York.

Garrick, John and Robin Usher. 2000. Flexible learning, contemporary work and enterprising selves. *Electronic Journal of Sociology*, 5(1).

Garsten, Christina. 1994. *Apple World: Core and Periphery in a Transnational Organizational Culture*. Doctoral Dissertation. Department of Social anthropology, Stockholm University. Stockholm: Almqvist & Wiksell International.

Garsten, Christina. 1999. Betwixt and between: Temporary employees as liminal subjects in flexible organizations. *Organization Studies*, 20(4): 601–617.

Garsten, Christina. 2002. Flex fads: New economy, new employees. In Ingalill Holmberg, Miriam Salzer-Mörling and Lars Strannegård, eds. *Stuck in the Future?: Tracing the 'New Economy'*. Stockholm: Book House Publishing, pp. 241–265.

Garsten, Christina. 2003. Colleague, competitor, or client: Social boundaries in flexible work arrangements. In Neil Paulsen and Tor Hernes, eds. *Managing Boundaries in Organizations: Multiple Perspectives*. Basingstoke: Palgrave Macmillan, pp. 244–261.

Garsten, Christina. 2004. 'Be a Gumby': The political technologies of employability in the temporary staffing business. In Christina Garsten and Kerstin Jacobsson, eds. *Learning to be Employable: New Agendas on Work, Employability and Learning in a Globalizing World*. Basingstoke: Palgrave Macmillan, pp. 152–171.

Garsten, Christina and Staffan Furusten. 2005. 'New' professionalism: Conditions for expertise in management consulting and temporary administrative staffing. In Staffan Furusten and Andreas Werr, eds. *Dealing with Confidence*. Copenhagen: Copenhagen Business Press, pp. 19–38.

Garsten, Christina and Jan Turtinen. 2000. 'Angels' and 'chameleons': The cultural construction of the flexible temporary employee in Sweden and the UK. In Bo Stråth, ed. *After Full Employment. European Discourses on Work and Flexibility*. Brussels: Peter Lang, pp. 161–198.

Garsten, Christina and Kerstin Jacobsson, eds. 2004. *Learning to be Employable: New Agendas on Work, Employability and Learning in a Globalizing World*. Basingstoke: Palgrave Macmillan.

Geertz, Clifford. 1973. In *The Interpretation of Cultures*. New York: Basic Books.

Goffman, Erving. 1959. *The Presentation of Self in Everyday Life*. New York, NY: Anchor Books.

Goffman, Erving. 1961. *Asylums: Essays on the Social Situation of Mental Patients and Other Inmates*. New York, NY: Anchor Books.

Goffman, Erving. 1963. *Stigma: Notes on the Management of Spoiled Identity*. Englewood Cliffs, NJ: Prentice-Hall.

Goffman, Erving. 1974. *Frame Analysis*. New York, NY: Harper Books.

Gottfried, Heidi. 1992. In the margins: Flexibility as a mode of regulation in the temporary help service industry. *Work, Employment and Society*, 6(3): 443–460.

Goudswaard, Anneke and Mattieu de Nanteuil. 2000. *Flexibility and Working Conditions: A Qualitative and Comparative Study in Seven EU Member States*. *European Foundation for the Improvement of Living and Working Conditions*.

Luxembourg, Office for Official Publications of the European Communities.

Grey, Chris. 1994. Career as a project of the self and labour process discipline. *Sociology*, 28(2): 479–497.

Grey, Chris. 2007. Management as a technical practice: Professionalization or responsibilization? *Systems Practice*, 10(6): 703–725.

Grey, Chris and Christina Garsten. 2001. Trust, control and post-bureaucracy. *Organization Studies*, 22(2): 229–250.

Grey, Chris and Christina Garsten. 2002. Organized and disorganized Utopias: An essay on presumption. In Martin Parker, ed. *Utopia and Organization* (Sociological Review Monograph, 50). Oxford: Blackwell, pp. 9–23.

Gusterson, Hugh. 1997. 'Studying up' revisited. *Political and Legal Anthropology Review*, 20(1): 114–119.

Hacking, Ian. 1986. Making up people. In Thomas C. Heller, Morton Sosna and David E. Wellbury. eds. *Reconstructing Individualism*. Stanford: Stanford University Press, pp. 222–236.

Hall, Elaine J. 1993. Smiling, deferring, and flirting: Doing gender by giving 'good service'. *Work and Occupations*, 20(4): 452–471.

Håkansson, Kristina and Tommy Isidorsson. 2007. Flexibility, stability and agency work: A comparison of the use of agency work in Sweden and the UK. In Furåker, Bengt, Kristina Håkansson and Jan C. Karlsson, eds. 2007. *Flexiblity and Stability in Working Life*. Basingstoke: Palgrave Macmillan, pp. 123–147.

Hall, Rodney B. och Thomas J. Biersteker. 2002. *The Emergence of Private Authority in Global Governance*. Cambridge: Cambridge University Press.

Hannerz, Ulf. 1987. The world in creolization. *Africa*, 57(4): 546–559.

Hannerz, Ulf. 1990. Cosmopolitans and locals in world culture. In Mike Featherstone, ed. *Global Culture: Nationalism, Globalization and Modernity*. London: Sage, pp. 237–251.

Hannerz, Ulf. 1992. *Cultural Complexity: Studies in the Social Organization of Meaning*. New York, NY: Columbia University Press.

Hannerz, Ulf. 1996. *Transnational Connections: Culture, People, Places*. London: Routledge.

Hannerz, Ulf. 1998. Transnational research. In H. Russell Barnard, ed. *Handbook of Methods in Cultural Anthropology*. Walnut Creek. CA: Altamira, pp. 235–258.

Hannerz, Ulf. 2004. *Foreign News*. Chicago, IL: University of Chicago Press.

Hannerz, Ulf. 2006. Studying down, up, sideways, through, backward, forward, away and at home: Reflections on the field worries of an expansive discipline. In Simon M. Coleman and Peter J. Collins, eds. *Locating the Field*. Oxford: Berg, pp. 23–41.

Hanson, Marika. 2004. *Det flexibla arbetets villkor: Om självförvaltandets kompetens*. Doctoral thesis, 127. Stockholm University, Department of Pedagogy. National Institute for Working Life, Worklife in Transition series, 8.

Harper, Douglas and Helene M. Lawson, eds. 2003. *The Cultural Study of Work*. Lanham: Rowman & Littlefield Publishers.

Harvey, David. 1989. *The Condition of Postmodernity*. Oxford: Blackwell.

Harvey, Michael, W. F. 2002. The Social Dialogue as a case of network governance: Lessons from the failure of the framework agreement on temporary agency work. University of Toronto: Department of Political Science. Paper presented to the First Annual Pan-European Conference on European Union Politics, Bordeaux, 26–28 September 2002.

Hasselström, Anna. 2003. *On and Off the Trading Floor. An Inquiry Into the Everyday Fashioning of Financial Market Knowledge*. Doctoral Dissertation. Stockholm University. Department of Social Anthropology.

Haunschild, Axel. 2004. Contingent work: The problem of disembeddedness and economic reembeddedness. *The International Review of Management Studies*, 15(1): 74–88.

Haunschild, Axel. 2003. Managing employment relationships in flexible labour markets: The case of German repertory theatres. *Human Relations*, 56(8): 899–929.

Henson, Kevin D. 1996. *Just a Temp*. Philadelphia, PA: Temple University Press.

Hepple, Bobb. 1993. United Kingdom. In R. Blanpain, ed. *Temporary Work and Labour Law of the European Community and Labour States*. Deventer: Kluwer Law and Taxation Publishers.

Hochschild, Arlie Russell. 1983. *The Managed Heart: Commercialization of Human Feeling*. Berkeley: University of California Press.

Hochshild, Arlie Russell. 1997. *The Time Bind: When Work Becomes Home and Home Becomes Work*. New York, NY: Metropolitan Books.

Hörning, Karl H., Anette Gerhard and Matthias Michailow. 1996. *Time Pioneers: Flexible Working Time and New Lifestyles*. Cambridge: Polity Press.

Hossfeld, Karen. 1990. 'Their logic against them': Contradictions in sex, race, and class in Silicon Valley. In Kathryn Ward, ed. *Women Workers and Global Restructuring*. Ithaca, NY: ILR Press, pp. 149–178.

Jacobsson, Kerstin and Geir A. Øygarden. 1999. Beredskapskulturen (The culture of preparedness). Unpublished manuscript. Dept of Sociology, Uppsala University.

Kalleberg, Arne L. 2000. Nonstandard employment relations: Part-time, temporary and contract work. *Annual Review of Sociology*, 26: 342–365.

Kalleberg, Arne L., Barbara F. Reskin, and Ken Hudson. 2000. Bad jobs in America: Standard and nonstandard employment relations and job quality in the United States. *American Sociological Review*, 65(2): 256–279.

Kalleberg, Arne L. and Peter V. Marsden. 2005. Externalizing organizational activities: Where and how U.S. establishments use employment intermediaries. *Socio-Economic review*, 3: 389–416.

Kärreman, Dan. 2001. The scripted organization: Dramaturgy from Burke to Baudrillard. In R. Westwood and S. Linstead, eds. *The Language of Organization*. London: Sage Publications, pp. 95–111.

Kärreman, Dan and Mats Alvesson. 2001. Making newsmakers: Conversational identity at work. *Organization Studies*, 22(1): 59–89.

Kedia, Simi and Peter Tufano. 2001. Adecco SA's acquisition of Olsten Corp. *Harvard Business School Cases*, 9–201–068.

Keenan, William J.F. 2001. Dress freedom: The personal and the political. In William J.F. Keenan, ed. *Dressed to Impress: Looking the Part*. Oxford: Berg, pp. 179–198

Kunda, Gideon and John van Maanen. 1999. Changing scripts at work: Managers and professionals. *Annals of the American Academy of Political and Social Science*, 561: 64–80.

Lash, Scott. 1994. Reflexivity and its doubles: Structure, aesthetics, community. In Ulrich Beck, Anthony Giddens and Scott Lash *Reflexive Modernization: Politics, Tradition and Aesthetics in the Modern Social Order*, Stanford: Stanford University Press, pp. 110–173.

Lash, Scott and John Urry. 1987. *The End of Organized Capitalism*. Cambridge, MA: Polity Press.

Lash, Scott and John Urry. 1994. *Economies of Signs and Space*. London: Sage.

Latour, Bruno. 1993. *We Have Never Been Modern* (C. Porter, Trans.). Cambridge, MA: Harvard University Press.

Littler, Craig R. 1982. *The Development of the Labour Process in Britain, Japan and USA*. London: Heinemann.

Lundmark, Lennart. 1993. *Tiden är bara ett ord*. Stockholm: Prisma.

Mangham, Iain L. and Michael A. Overington. 1987. *Organizations as Theatre*. Chichester, NY: Wiley.

Martin, Emily. 1994. *Flexible Bodies: Tracking Immunity in American Culture – From the Days of Polio to the Age of AIDS*. Boston, MA: Beacon Press.

Martin, Joanne, Kathy Knopoff and Christine Beckman. 2000. Bounded emotionality at the body shop. In Stephen Fineman, ed. *Emotion in Organizations*. London: Sage, pp. 115–139.

McAllister, Jean. 1998. Sisyphus at work in the warehouse: Temporary employment in Greenville, South Carolina. In Kathleen Barker and Kathleen Christensen, eds. *Contingent Work: American Employment in Transition*. Ithaca, NY: ILR Press, pp. 221–242.

McGee, Micki. 2005. *Self-Help, Inc.: Makeover Culture in American Life*. Oxford: Oxford University Press.

Meyer, Stephen. 1981. The five-dollar day: Labor management and social control in the Ford Motor Co., 1908–1921. Albany, NY: State University of New York Press.

Meyer, John W. and Ronald L. Jepperson. 2000. The 'actors' of modern society: The cultural construction of social agency, *Sociological Theory*, 18(1): 100–121.

Miller, Peter and Nikolas Rose. 1995. Production, identity, and democracy. *Theory and Society*, 24(3): 427–467.

Moeran, Brian. 2005. *The Business of Ethnography: Strategic Exchanges, People and Organizations*. Oxford: Berg.

Munro, Ronald. 1998. Ethics and accounting: The dual technologies of self. In Martin Parker, ed. *Ethics and Organizations*. London: Sage.

Noon, Mike and Paul Blyton. 1997. *The Realities of Work*. Basingstoke: Macmillan.

Nyberg Sörensen, Ninna and Karen Fog Olvig, eds. 2002. *Work and Migration: Life and Livelihoods in a Globalizing World.* London: Routledge.

OECD. 1995. *Employment Outlook.* July 1995. Paris: OECD.

OECD. 1997. *Labour Market Policies: New Challenges. Enhancing the Effectiveness of Active Labour Market Policies: A Streamlined Public Employment Service.* OECD/GD(97)161.

Offe, Claus. 1985. *Disorganized Capitalism: Contemporary Transformations of Work and Politics.* Cambridge, MA: MIT Press.

Ong, Aihwa. 1999. *Flexible Citizenship: The Cultural Logics of Transnationality.* Durham, NC: Duke University Press.

Ong, Aihwa. 2006. *Neoliberalism as Exception: Mutations in Citizenship and Sovereignty.* Durham, NC: Duke University Press.

Ortner, Sherry. 1997. Fieldwork in the postcommunity. In Sandra Bamford and Joel Robbins, eds. *Anthropology and Humanism* 22(1): 61–80 (special issue on Fieldwork in the Era of Globalization).

Parker, Robert E. 1994. *Flesh Peddlers and Warm Bodies: The Temporary Help Industry and Its Workers.* New Brunswick, NJ: Rutgers University Press.

Peck, Jamie. 2002. Labor, zapped/growth, restored? Three moments of neoliberal restructuring in the American labor market. *Journal of Economic Geography*, 23(2): 179–220.

Peck, Jamie A. and Nikolas Theodore. 2002. Temped out? Rhetoric, labor regulation and economic restructuring in the temporary Staffing Business. *Economic and Industrial Democracy*, 23(2): 143–175.

Peck, Jamie A. and Nikolas Theodore. 2007. Flexible recession: The temporary staffing industry and mediated work in the United States. *Cambridge Journal of Economics*, 31(2): 171–192.

Pfeffer, J. and J. N Baron. 1988. Taking the workers back out: Recent trends in the structuring of employment. In B. M. Staw and L. L. Cummings, eds. *Research in Organizational Behavior.* Greenwich, CT: JAI Press, pp. 257–303.

Pink, Daniel H. 2001. *Free Agent Nation: How America's New Independent Workers Are Transforming the Way We Live.* New York, NY: Warner Books.

Piore, Michael J. and Charles F. Sabel. 1984. *The Second Industrial Divide: Possibilities for Prosperity.* New York, NY: Basic Books.

Pollard, S. 1965. *The Genesis of Modern Management: A Study of the Industrial Revolution in Great Britain.* Harmondsworth: Penguin.

Pollert, Anna. 2007. Britain's flexible labour force: New barriers to individual employment rights. In Bengt Furåker, Kristina Håkansson and Jan C. Karlsson, eds. *Flexiblity and Stability in Working Life.* Basingstoke: Palgrave Macmillan, pp. 42–62.

Power, Michael. 1997. *The Audit Society: Rituals of Verification.* Oxford: Oxford University Press.

Rabinow, Paul. 2003. *Anthropos Today: Reflections on Modern Equipment.* Princeton, NJ: Princeton University Press.

Rabinow, Paul. 2005. Midst anthropology's problems. In Aihwa Ong and Stephen J. Collier, eds. *Global Assemblages: Technology, Politics, and Ethics as Anthropological Problems.* Malden, MA: Blackwell, pp. 40–53.

Reich, Robert B. 1992. *The Work of Nations.* New York, NY: Vintage Books.

Rifkin, Jeremy. 1995. *The End of Work: The Decline of the Global Labor Force and the Dawn of the Post-Market Era*. New York, NY: Tarcher/Putnam.

Riles, Annelise. 2000. *The Network Inside Out*. Ann Arbor, MI: The University of Michigan Press.

Robinson, Peter. 1999. Explaining the relationship between flexible employment and labour market regulation. In Alan. Felstead and Nick Jewson, eds. *Global Trends in Flexible Labour*. Basingstoke: Macmillan, pp. 84–99.

Rogers, Jacky K. 1995. 'Just a temp': Experience and structure of alienation in temporary clerical employment. *Work and Occupation*, 22(2): 137–166.

Rogers, Jacky K. 2000. *Temps: The Many Facets of the Changing Workplace*. Ithaca, NY: Cornell University Press.

Rogers, Richard M. 1996. *Temping: The Insider's Guide*. New York, NY: Macmillan.

Rose, Nikolas. 1999. *Powers of Freedom: Reframing Political Thought*. Cambridge: Cambridge University Press.

Rosenau, James N. 2003. *Distant Proximities: Dynamics beyond Globalization*. Princeton, NJ: Princeton University Press.

Sassen, Saskia. 1998. *Globalization and Its Discontents*, New York, NY: The New Press.

Scott, Robert A. 1969. *The Making of Blind Men: A Study of Adult Socialization*. New York, NY: Russell Sage Foundation.

Selznick, Philip. 1948. Foundations of the theory of organizations. *Sociological Review*, 13(1): 25–35.

Sennett, Richard. 1998. *The Corrosion of Character: The Personal Consequences of Work in the New Capitalism*. New York, NY: W. W. Norton.

Sennett, Richard. 2006. *The Culture of the New Capitalism*. New Haven, CT: Yale University Press.

Shore, Cris and Susan Wright. 2000. Coercive accountability: The rise of audit culture in higher education. In M. Strathern, ed. *Audit Cultures: Anthropological Studies in Accountability, Ethics and the Academy*. London: Routledge, pp. 57–89.

Simmel, Georg 1950 (1908). The stranger. In Kurt Wolff (Trans.). *The Sociology of Georg Simmel*. New York, NY: Free Press, pp. 402–408.

Smart, Alan and Josephine Smart, eds. 2005. *Petty Capitalists and Globalization: Flexibility, Entrepreneurship, and Economic Development*. Albany, NY: State University of New York Press.

Smith, Vicki. 1998. The fractured world of the temporary worker: Power, participation, and fragmentation of the contemporary workplace. *Social Problems*, 45: 1–20.

SOU. 1997: 58. *Personaluthyrning*. Arbetsmarknadsdepartementet.

Stinchcombe, Arthur L. 1965. Social structure and organizations. In James G. March, ed. *Handbook of Organizations*. Chicago: Rand McNally, pp. 142–193.

Stinchcombe, Arthur. 1990. Work institutions and the sociology of everyday life. In Kai Erikson and Steven Peter Vallas, eds. *The Nature of Work: Sociological Perspectives*. New Haven, CT: Yale University Press.

Stoller, Paul. 1997. Globalising method: The problems of doing ethnography in transnational spaces. *Anthropology and Humanism*, 22(1): 81–94 (special issue on Fieldwork in the Era of Globalization, eds. Sandra Bamford and Joel Robbins).

Storrie, Donald. 2002. *Temporary Agency Work in the European Union*. Dublin. European Foundation for the Improvement of Living and Working Conditions.

Strange, Susan. 1996. *The Retreat of the State: The Diffusion of Power in the World Economy*. Cambridge: Cambridge University Press.

Strathern, Marilyn. 1995. The nice thing about culture is that everyone has it. In M. Strathern, ed. *Shifting Contexts*. London: Routledge, pp. 153–176.

Stråth, Bo, ed. 2000. *After Full Employment. European Discourses on Work and Flexibility*. Brussels: Peter Lang.

Supiot, Alain. 2001. *Beyond Employment: Changes in Work and the Future of Labour Law in Europe*. Oxford: Oxford University Press.

Svensson, Birgitta. 1993. *Bortom all ära och redlighet*. Nordiska museets handlingar 114.

Sweeney, Sean. 2006. *Temporary Agency Work in the United States*. Dublin: European Foundation for the Improvement of Living and Working Conditions.

Thompson, Edward P. 1967. Time, work-discipline and industrial capitalism. *Past and Present*, 38(1): 56–97.

Tilly, Charles. 1999. *Durable Inequality*. Berkeley: University of California Press.

Vosko, Leah F. 2000. *Temporary Work: The Gendered Rise of a Precarious Employment Relationship*. Toronto: Toronto University Press.

Walsh, Janet. 1997. Employment systems in transition? A comparative analysis of Britain and Australia. *Work, Employment & Society* 11(1): 1–25.

Walter, Lars. 2005. *Som hand i handske: En studie av matchning i ett personaluthyrningsföretag*. Doctoral thesis. Handelshögskolan Göteborg. Bokförlaget BAS.

Weich, Karl E. 1979[1969]. *The Social Psychology of Organizing*. New York, NY: Random House.

Weinert, Patricia, Michèle Baukens, Partick Bollérot, Marina Pineschi-Gapènne and Ulrich Walwei, eds. 2001. *Employability. From Theory to Practice*. London: Transaction Publishers.

Wulff, Helena. 1998. *Ballet Across Borders. Career and Culture in the World of Dancers*. Oxford: Berg.

Wulff, Helena. 2002. Yo-yo fieldwork: Mobility and time in a multi-local study of dance in Ireland, *Anthropological Journal on European Cultures* (issue on Shifting Grounds: Experiments in Doing Ethnography), 11: 117–136.

Index

DATE DUE